Lady Magnus

Jewish Portraits

Lady Magnus

Jewish Portraits

ISBN/EAN: 9783743311329

Manufactured in Europe, USA, Canada, Australia, Japa

Cover: Foto ©Thomas Meinert / pixelio.de

Manufactured and distributed by brebook publishing software
(www.brebook.com)

Lady Magnus

Jewish Portraits

JEWISH PORTRAITS

BY

LADY MAGNUS

AUTHOR OF
'OUTLINES OF JEWISH HISTORY,' 'ABOUT THE JEWS
SINCE BIBLE TIMES,' ETC.

Second Revised and Enlarged Edition

LONDON
Published by DAVID NUTT
in the STRAND
1897

'THESE, TO HIS MEMORY'

FEBRUARY 7 : JANUARY 11

PREFACE

THE papers which form this volume have
already appeared in the pages of *Good Words,
Macmillan's Magazine, The National Review,*
and *The Spectator,* and are reprinted with the
very kindly given permission of the editors.
The Frontispiece is reproduced through the
kindness of the proprietors of *Good Words.*

I fancy that there is enough of family likeness, and I hope there is enough of friendly
interest, in these Jewish portraits to justify
their re-appearance in a little gallery to themselves.

KATIE MAGNUS.

CONTENTS

	PAGE
JEHUDAH HALEVI,	1
THE STORY OF A STREET,	24
HEINRICH HEINE: A PLEA,	32
DANIEL DERONDA AND HIS JEWISH CRITICS,	57
MANASSEH BEN ISRAEL,	68
CHARITY IN TALMUDIC TIMES,	90
MOSES MENDELSSOHN,	109
THE NATIONAL IDEA IN JUDAISM,	147
THE STORY OF A FALSE PROPHET,	158
NOW AND THEN: A COMPOSITE SKETCH,	177

JEWISH PORTRAITS

JEHUDAH HALEVI

PHYSICIAN AND POET

In the far-off days, when religion was not a habit, but an emotion, there lived a little-known poet who solved the pathetic puzzle of how to sing the Lord's song in a strange land. Minor poets of the period in plenty had essayed a like task, leaving a literature the very headings of which are strange to uninstructed ears. '*Piyutim*,' '*Selichoth*': what meaning do these words convey to most of us? And yet they stand for songs of exile, sung by patient generations of men who tell a monotonous tale of mournful times—

> 'When ancient griefs
> Are closely veiled
> In recent shrouds,'

as one of the anonymous host expresses it. For the writers were of the race of the traditional Sweet Singer, and their lot was

A

cast in those picturesquely disappointing Middle Ages, too close to the chivalry of the time to appreciate its charm. One pictures these comparatively cultured pariahs, these gaberdined, degenerate descendants of seers and prophets, looking out from their ghettoes on a world which, for all the stir and bustle of barbaric life, was to them as desolate and as bare of promise of safe resting-place as when the waters covered it, and only the tops of the mountains appeared. One sees them now as victims, and now as spectators, but never as actors in that strange show, yet always, we fancy, realising the barbarism, and with that undoubting faith of theirs in the ultimate dawning of a perfect day, seeming to regard the long reign of brute force, of priestcraft, and of ignorance as phases of mis-rule, which, like unto manifold others, should pass whilst they would endure.

> ' A race that has been tested
> And tried through fire and water,
> Is surely prized by Thee,'

cries out a typical bard, with, perhaps, a too-conscious tone of martyrdom, and a decided tendency to clutch at the halo. The attitude is altogether a trifle arrogant and stolid and defiant to superficial criticism, but yet one for which a deeper insight will find excuses. The complacency is not quite self-complacency, the pride is impersonal, and so, though provoking, is pathetic too. Something of the old longing which, with a sort of satisfied negation, claimed 'honour and glory,' 'not unto us,' but unto 'the Name,' seems to find expression again in the unrhymed and often unrhythmical compositions of these patient poets of the *Selicha*. Their poetry, perhaps, goes some way towards explaining their patience, for, undoubtedly, there is no doggedness like that of men who at will, and by virtue of their own thoughts, can soar above circumstances and surroundings. 'Vulgar minds,' says a last-century poet, truly enough, 'refuse or crouch beneath their load,' and inevitably such will collapse under a pressure which the cultivated will endure, and 'bear without repining.' The ills to which flesh is heir will generally be best and most bravely borne by those to whom the flesh is not all in all; as witness Heine, whose voice rose at its sweetest, year after year, from his mattress grave. That there never was a time in all their history when the lusts of the flesh were a whole and satisfying ambition to the Jew, or when the needs of the body bounded his desires, may account in some degree for that marvellous capacity for suffering which the race has evinced.

These rugged *Piyutim*, for over a thousand years, come in from most parts of the continent of Europe as a running commentary on its laws, suggesting a new reading for the old significant connection between a country's lays and its legislation, and supplying an illustration to Charles Kingsley's dictum, that 'the literature of a nation is its autobiography.' *Selicha* (from the Hebrew, סליחה) means literally forgiveness, and to forgive and to be forgiven is the burden and the refrain of most of the so-called Penitential Poems (*Selichoth*), whose theme is of sorrows and persecutions past telling, almost past praying about. *Piyut* (derived from the Greek ποιητής) in early Jewish writings stood for the poet himself, and later on it was applied as a generic name for his compositions. From the second to the eighth century there is decidedly more suggestion of martyrdom than of minstrelsy in these often unsigned and always unsingable sonnets of the synagogue, and especially about the contributions from France, and subsequently from Germany, to the liturgical literature of the Middle Ages, there is a far too prevailing note of the swan's song for cheerful reading. Happier in their circumstances than the rest of their European co-religionists, the Spanish writers sing, for the most part, in clearer and higher strains, and it is they who towards the close of the tenth century, first add something of the grace and charm of metrical versification to the hitherto crude and rough style of composition which had sufficed. Even about the prose of these Spanish authors there is many a light and happy touch, and, not unseldom, in the voluminous and somewhat verbose literature, we come across a short story (*midrash*) or a pithy saying, with salt enough of wit or of pathos about it to make its preservation through the ages quite comprehensible.

Hep, Hep, was the dominant note in the European concert, when at the beginning of the twelfth century our poet was born. France, Italy, Germany, Bohemia, and Greece had each been, at different times within the hundred years which had just closed, the scene of terrible persecutions. In Spain alone, under the mild sway of the Ommeyade Kaliphs, there had been a tolerably long entr'acte in the 'fifteen hundred year tragedy' that the Jewish race was enacting, and there, in old Castille, whilst Alfonso VI. was king, Jehudah Halevi passed his childhood. Although in 1085 Alfonso was already presiding over an important confederation of Catholic States, yet at the beginning of the twelfth century the Arab supremacy in Spain was still comparatively unshaken, and

its influence, social and political, over its
Jewish subjects was still paramount. Perhaps
the one direction in which that impressionable race was least perceptibly affected by
its Arab experiences was in its literature.
And remembering how very distinctly in the
elder days of art the influence of Greek
thought is traceable in Jewish philosophy, it
is strange to note with these authors of the
Middle Ages, who write as readily in Arabic
as in Hebrew, that, though the hand is the
hand of Esau, the voice remains unmistak-
ably the voice of Jacob. Munk dwells on
this remarkable distinction in the poetry of
the period, and with some natural preference
perhaps, strives to account for it in the wide
divergence of the Hebrew and Arabic sources
of inspiration. The poetry of the Jews he
roundly declares to be universal, and that of
the Arabs egotistic in its tendency; the sons
of the desert finding subjects for their Muse
in traditions of national glory and in dreams
of material delight, whilst the descendants
of prophets turn to the records of their own
ancestry, and find their themes in remorseful
memories, and in unselfish and unsensual
hopes. With the Jewish poet, past and
future are alike uncoloured by personal desire,
and even the sins and sufferings of his race
he enshrines in song. If it be good, as a

modern writer has declared it to be, that a nation should commemorate its defeats, certainly no race has ever been richer in such subjects, or has shown itself more willing, in ritual and rhyme, to take advantage of them.

Whilst the leaders of society, the licentious crusader and the celibate monk, were stumbling so sorely in the shadow of the Cross, and whilst the rank and file throughout Europe were steeped in deepest gloom of densest ignorance and superstition, the lamp of learning, handed down from generation to generation of despised Jews, was still being carefully trimmed, and was burning at its brightest among the little knot of philosophers and poets in Spain. Alcharisi, the commentator and critic of the circle, gives, for his age, a curiously high standard of the qualifications essential to the sometimes lightly bestowed title of author. 'A poet,' he says, '(1) must be perfect in metre; (2) his language of classic purity; (3) the subject of his poem worthy of the poet's best skill, and calculated to instruct and to elevate mankind; (4) his style must be full of "lucidity" and free from every obscure or foreign expression; (5) he must never sacrifice sense to sound; (6) he must add infinite care and patience to his gift of genius, never submitting crude work to the world;

and (7) lastly, he must neither parade all he knows nor offer the winnowings of his harvest.'

These seem sufficiently severe conditions even to nineteenth-century judgment, but Jehudah Halevi, say his admirers and even his contemporaries, fulfilled them all.

That a man should be judged by his peers gives a promise of sound and honest testimony, and if such judgment be accepted as final, then does Halevi hold high rank indeed among men and poets. One of the first things that strike an intruder into this old-world literary circle is the curious absence of those small rivalries and jealousies which we of other times and manners look instinctively to find. Such records as remain to us make certainly less amusing reading than some later biographies and autobiographies afford, but, on the other hand, it has a unique interest of its own, to come upon authentic traces of such susceptible beings as authors, all living in the same set and with a limited range both of subjects and of readers, who yet live together in harmony, and interchange sonnets and epigrams curiously free from every suggestion of envy, hatred, or uncharitableness. There is, in truth, a wonderful freshness of sentiment about these gentle old scholars. They say pretty things to and of each other in almost school-girl fashion. 'I pitch my tent in thy heart,' exclaims one as he sets out on a journey. More poetically Halevi expresses a similar sentiment to a friend of his (Ibn Giat):

> 'If to the clouds thy boldness wings its flight,
> Within our hearts, thou ne'er art out of sight.'

Writes another (Moses Aben Ezra), and he was a philosopher and grammarian to boot, one not to be lightly suspected of sentimentality, 'Our hearts were as one : now parted from thee, my heart is divided into two.' Halevi was the absent friend in this instance, and he begins his response as warmly :—

> 'How can I rest when we are absent one from
>   another?
> Were it not for the glad hope of thy return
> The day which tore thee from me
> Would tear me from all the world.'

Or the note changes : some disappointment or disillusion is hinted at, and under its influence our tender-hearted poet complains to this same sympathetic correspondent, 'I was asked, Hast thou sown the seed of friendship? My answer was, Alas, I did, but the seed did not thrive.'

It is altogether the strangest, soberest little picture of sweetness and light, showing beneath the gaudy, tawdry phantasmagoria of

the age. Rub away the paint and varnish
from the hurrying host of crusaders, from the
confused crowd of dreary, deluded rabble, and
there they stand like a 'restored' group, these
tuneful, unworldly sages, 'toiling, rejoicing,
sorrowing,' with Jehudah Halevi, poet and
physician, as central figure. For, loyal to the
impulse which in times long past had turned
Akiba into a herdsman and had induced Hillel
in his youth and poverty to 'hire himself out
wherever he could find a job,'[1] which, in the
time to come, was to make of Maimonides a
diamond-cutter, and of Spinoza an optician,
Halevi compounded simples as conscientiously
as he composed sonnets, and was more of
doctor than of poet by profession. He was
true to those traditions and instincts of his race,
which, through all the ages, had recognised
the dignity of labour and had inclined to use
literature as a staff rather than as a crutch.
His prescriptions were probably such as the
Pharmacopœia of to-day might hardly approve,
and the spirit in which he prescribed, one
must own, is perhaps also a little out of date.
Here is a grace just before physic which
brings to one's mind the advice given by a
famous divine of the muscular Christianity
school to his young friend at Oxford, 'Work
hard—as for your degree, leave it to God.'

[1] Talmud, Yoma 356.

'God grant that I may rise again,
Nor perish by Thine anger slain.
This draught that I myself combine,
What is it? Only Thou dost know
If well or ill, if swift or slow,
Its parts shall work upon my pain.
Ay, of these things, alone is Thine
The knowledge. All my faith I place,
Not in my craft, but in Thy grace.'[1] (1)

Halevi's character, however, was far enough removed from that which an old author has defined as 'pious and painefull.' He 'entered the courts with gladness': his religion being of a healthy, happy, natural sort, free from all affectations, and with no taint either of worldliness or of other-worldliness to be discerned in it. Perhaps our poet was not entirely without that comfortable consciousness of his own powers and capabilities which, in weaker natures, turns its seamy side to us as conceit, nor altogether free from that impatience of 'fools' which seems to be another of the temptations of the gifted. This rather ill-tempered little extract which we are honest enough to append appears to indicate as much :—

'Lo ! my light has pierced to the dark abyss,
I have brought forth gems from the gloomy mine;

---

[1] The extracts marked thus (1) were done into verse from the German of Geiger, by the late Amy Levy.

Now the fools would see them! I ask you this:
Shall I fling my pearls down before the swine?
From the gathered cloud shall the raindrops flow
To the barren land where no fruit can grow?' (1)

The little grumble is characteristic, but in actual fact no land was 'barren' to his hopeful, sunny temperament. In the 'morning he sowed his seed, and in the evening he withheld not his hand,' and from his 'gathered clouds,' the raindrops fell rainbow-tinted. The love songs, which a trustworthy edition tells us were written to his wife, are quite as beautiful in their very different way as an impassioned elegy he wrote when death claimed his friend, Aben Ezra, or as the famous ode he composed on Jerusalem. Halevi wrote prose too, and a bulky volume in Arabic is in existence, which sets forth the history of a certain Bulan, king of the Khozars, who reigned, the antiquarians agree, about the beginning of the eighth century, over a territory situate on the shores of the Caspian Sea. This Bulan would seem to have been of a hesitating, if not of a sceptical, turn of mind in religious matters. Honestly anxious to be correct in his opinions, his anxiety becomes intensified by means of a vision, and he finally summons representative followers of Moses, of Jesus, and of Mahomet, to discuss in his presence the tenets of their masters. These chosen doctors of divinity

argue at great length, and the Jewish Rabbi
is said to have best succeeded in satisfying
the anxious scruples of the king. The same
authorities tell us that Bulan became an
earnest convert to Judaism, and commenced
in his own person a Jewish dynasty which
endured for more than two centuries. Over
these more or less historic facts Halevi casts
the glamour of his genius, and makes, at any
rate, a very readable story out of them, which
incidentally throws some valuable side-lights
on his own way of regarding things. Unluckily,
side-lights are all we possess, in place of the
electric illuminating fashion of the day. Those
copious details, which our grandchildren seem
likely to inherit concerning all and sundry of
this generation, are wholly wanting to us, the
earlier heirs of time. Of Halevi, as of greater
poets, who have lived even nearer to our own
age, history speaks neither loudly nor in
chorus. Yet, for our consolation, there is the
reflection that the various and varying records
of 'Thomas's ideal John : never the real John,
nor John's John, but often very unlike either,'
may, in truth, help us but little to a right
comprehension of the 'real John, known
only to His Maker.' Once get at a man's
ideals, it has been well said, and the rest is
easy. And thus though our facts are but few
and fragmentary concerning the man of whom

one admirer quaintly says that, 'created in
the image of God' could in his case stand
for literal description, yet may we, by means
of his ideals, arrive perhaps at a juster conception of Halevi's charming personality than
did we possess the very pen with which he
wrote and the desk at which he sat and the
minutest and most authentic particulars as to
his wont of using both.

His ideal of religion was expressed in every
practical detail of daily life.

> 'When I remove from Thee, O God,
>   I die whilst I live ; but when
>   I cleave to Thee, I live in death.'[1]

These three lines indicate the sentiment
of Judaism, and might almost serve as sufficient
sample of Halevi's simple creed, for, truth to
tell, the religion of the Jews does not concern
itself greatly with the ideal, being of a practical
rather than of an emotional sort, rigid as to
practice, but tolerant over theories, and inquiring less as to a man's belief than as to his
conduct. Work — steady, cheerful, untiring
work—was perhaps Halevi's favourite form of
praise. Still, being a poet, he sings, and, like
the birds, in divers strains, with happy, unconscious effort. Only ' For Thy songs, O God !'
he cries, 'my heart is a harp'; and truly

[1] From Atonement Service.

enough, in some of these ancient Hebrew
hymns, the stately intensity of which it is
impossible to reproduce, we seem to hear
clearly the human strings vibrate. The
truest faith, the most living hope, the widest
charity, is breathed forth in them; and they
have naturally been enshrined by his fellow-
believers in the most sacred parts of their
liturgy, quotations from which would here
obviously be out of place. Some dozen lines
only shall be given, and these chosen in
illustration of the universality of the Jewish
hope. 'Where can I find Thee, O God?'
the poet questions; and there is wonderfully
little suggestion of reserved places about the
answer :—

'Lord! where art Thou to be found?
Hidden and high is Thy home.
And where shall we find Thee not?
Thy glory fills the world.
Thou art found in my heart,
And at the uttermost ends of the earth.
A refuge for the near,
For the far, a trust.

'The universe cannot contain Thee;
How then a temple's shrine?
Though Thou art raised above men
On Thy high and lofty throne,
Yet art Thou near unto them
In their spirit and in their flesh.

Who can say he has not seen Thee?
When lo ! the heavens and their host
Tell of Thy fear, in silent testimony.

'I sought to draw near to Thee.
With my whole heart I sought Thee.
And when I went out to meet Thee,
To meet me, Thou wast ready on the road.
In the wonders of Thy might
And in Thy holiness I have beheld Thee.
Who is there that should not fear Thee?
The yoke of Thy kingdom is for ever and for all,
Who is there that should not call upon Thee?
Thou givest unto all their food.'

Concerning Halevi's ideal of love and marriage we may speak at greater length; and on these subjects one may remark that our poet's ideal was less individual than national. Mixing intimately among men who, as a matter of course, bestowed their fickle favours on several wives, and whose poetic notion of matrimony—on the prosaic we will not touch—was a houri-peopled Paradise, it is perhaps to the credit of the Jews that this was one of the Arabian customs which, with all their susceptibility, they were very slow to adopt. Halevi, as is the general faithful fashion of his race, all his life long loved one only, and clave to her—a 'dove of rarest worth, and sweet exceedingly,' as in one of his poems he declares her to be. The test of poetry, Goethe somewhere says, is the substance which remains when the poetry is reduced to prose. When the poetry has been yet further reduced by successive processes of translation, the test becomes severe. We fancy, though, that there is still some considerable residuum about Halevi's songs to his old-fashioned love—his Ophrah, as he calls her in some of them. Here is one when they are likely to be parted for a while :—

'So we must be divided ; sweetest, stay,
 Once more, mine eyes would seek thy glance's
  light.
At night I shall recall thee : Thou, I pray,
 Be mindful of the days of our delight.
Come to me in my dreams, I ask of thee,
And even in my dreams be gentle unto me.

'If thou shouldst send me greeting in the grave,
 The cold breath of the grave itself were sweet ;
Oh, take my life, my life, 'tis all I have,
 If it should make thee live, I do entreat.
I think that I shall hear when I am dead,
The rustle of thy gown, thy footsteps overhead.' (1)

And another, which reads like a marriage hymn :—

  'A dove of rarest worth
  And sweet exceedingly;
  Alas, why does she turn
  And fly so far from me?

B

In my fond heart a tent,
Should aye preparèd be.
My poor heart she has caught
With magic spells and wiles.
I do not sigh for gold,
But for her mouth that smiles ;
Her hue it is so bright,
She half makes blind my sight,

 . . . .

The day at last is here
Fill'd full of love's sweet fire ;
The twain shall soon be one,
Shall stay their fond desire.
Ah ! would my tribe could chance
On such deliverance.' (1)

On a first reading, these last two lines strike
one as oddly out of place in a love poem.
But as we look again, they seem to suggest,
that in a nature so full and wholesome as
Halevi's, love did not lead to a selfish forget-
fulness, nor marriage mean a joy which could
hold by its side no care for others. Rather to
prove that love at its best does not narrow
the sympathies, but makes them widen and
broaden out to enfold the less fortunate under
its happy, brooding wings. And though at
the crowning moment of his life Halevi could
spare a tender thought for his 'tribe,' with
very little right could the foolish, favourite
epithet of 'tribalism' be flung at him, and
with even less of justice at his race. In truth,

they were 'patriots' in the sorriest, sincerest sense—this dispossessed people, who owned not an inch of the lands wherein they wandered, from the east unto the west. It is prejudice or ignorance maybe, but certainly it is not history, which sees the Jews as any but the faithfullest of citizens to [their adopted States ; faithful, indeed, often to the extent of forgetting, save in set and prayerful phrases, the lost land of their fathers. Here is a typical national song of the twelfth century, in which no faintest echo of regret or of longing for other glories, other shrines, can be discerned :—

'I found that words could ne'er express
 The half of all its loveliness ;
 From place to place I wander'd wide,
 With amorous sight unsatisfied,
 Till last I reach'd all cities' queen,
   Tolaitola [1] the fairest seen.

   .   .   .   .   .

 Her palaces that show so bright
 In splendour, shamed the starry height,
 Whilst temples in their glorious sheen
 Rivall'd the glories that had been ;
 With earnest reverent spirit there,
 The pious soul breathes forth its prayer.'

The 'earnest reverent spirit' may be a little out of drawing now, but that 'fairest

---

[1] Hebrew for Toledo.

city seen' of the Spanish poet,[1] might well
stand for the London or Paris of to-day in
the well-satisfied, cosmopolitan affections of
an ordinary Englishman or Frenchman of the
Jewish faith. And which of us may blame
this adaptability, this comfortable inconstancy
of content? Widows and widowers remarry,
and childless folks, it is said, grow quite
foolishly fond of adopted kin. With practical
people the past is past, and to the prosperous
nothing comes more easy than forgetting.
After all—

' What can you do with people when they are dead?
But if you are pious, sing a hymn and go;
Or, if you are tender, heave a sigh and go,
But go by all means, and permit the grass
To keep its green fend 'twixt them and you.'[2]

In the long centuries since Jerusalem fell
there has been time and to spare for the green
grass to wither into dusty weeds above those
desolate dead whose 'place knows them no
more.' That Halevi with his 'poetic heart,'
which is a something different from the most
metrical of poetic imaginations, cherished a
closer ideal of patriotism than some of his
brethren may not be denied. 'Israel among
the nations,' he writes, 'is as the heart among
the limbs.' He was the loyalest of Spanish

---

[1] Alcharisi.   [2] E. B. Browning.

subjects, yet Jerusalem was ever to him, in sober fact, ' the city of the world.'

In these learned latter days, the tiniest crumbs of tradition have been so eagerly pounced upon by historians to analyse and argue over, that we are almost left in doubt whether the very A B C of our own history may still be writ in old English characters. The process which has bereft the bogy uncle of our youthful belief of his hump, and all but transformed the Bluebeard of the British throne into a model monarch, has not spared to set its puzzling impress on the few details which have come down to us concerning Halevi. Whether the love-poems, some eight hundred in number, were all written to his wife, is now questioned; whether 1086 or 1105 is the date of his birth, and if Toledo or Old Castille be his birthplace, is contested. Whether he came to a peaceful end, or was murdered by wandering Arabs, is left doubtful, since both the year of his death [1] and the manner of it are stated in different ways by different authorities, among whom it is hard to choose. Whether, indeed, he ever visited the Holy City, whether he beheld it with ' actual sight or sight of faith,' is greatly and gravely debated ; but amidst all this bewildering dust of doubt that the researches of wise

[1] No authority gives it later than 1140.

commentators have raised, the central fact of
his life is left to us undisputed. The realities
they meddle with, but the ideals, happily,
they leave to us undimmed. All at least
agree, that 'she whom the Rabbi loved was
a poor woe-begone darling, a moving picture
of desolation, and her name was Jerusalem.'
There is a consensus of opinion among the
critics that this often-quoted saying of Heine's
was only a poetical way of putting a literal
and undoubted truth. On this subject, indeed, our poet has only to speak for himself.

'Oh ! city of the world, most chastely fair ;
  In the far west, behold I sigh for thee.
  And in my yearning love I do bethink me,
  Of bygone ages ; of thy ruined fane,
  Thy vanish'd splendour of a vanish'd day.
  Oh ! had I eagles' wings I'd fly to thee,
  And with my falling tears make moist thine earth.
  I long for thee ; what though indeed thy kings
  Have passed for ever ; that where once uprose
  Sweet balsam-trees the serpent makes his nest.
  O that I might embrace thy dust, the sod
  Were sweet as honey to my fond desire !' (1)

Fifty translations cannot spoil the true ring
in such fervid words as these. And in a
world so sadly full of 'fond desires,' destined
to remain for ever unfulfilled, it is pleasant to
know that Halevi accomplished his. He un-
questionably travelled to Palestine ; whether

his steps were stayed short of Jerusalem we know not, but he undoubtedly reached the shores, and breathed 'the air of that land which makes men wise,' as in loving hyperbole a more primitive patriot[1] expresses it.

And seeing how that 'the Lord God doth like a printer who setteth the letters backward,'[2] there is small cause, perchance, for grieving in that the breath our poet drew in the land of his dreams was the breath not of life but of death.

[1] Rabbi Seira.

[2] 'The Lord God doth like a printer who setteth the letters backward; we see and feel well His setting, but the print we shall see yonder in the life to come.'— Luther's *Table Talk*.

THE STORY OF A STREET

To the ear and eye that can find sermons in
stones, streets, one would fancy, must be
brimful of suggestive stories. There might
be differences of course. From a stone of
the polished pebble variety, for instance, one
could only predict smooth platitudes, and the
romance in a block of regulation stucco would
possibly turn out a trifle prosaic. But the
right stone and the right street will always
have an eloquence of their own for the right
listener or lounger, and certain crumbling old
tenements which were carted away as rubbish
some few years ago in Frankfort must have
been rarely gifted in this line. 'Words of
fire,' and 'written in blood,' would, in truth,
have no parabolic meaning, if the stones of
that ancient *Judengasse* suddenly took to
story-telling. A long record of sorrow, and
wrong, and squalid romance, would be unfolded, and, inasmuch as the sorrows have
been healed and the wrongs have been
righted, it may not be uninteresting to look
for a moment at the picturesque truths that

lie hidden under that squalid romance, which, like a mist, hung for centuries over the Jews' quarter.

The very first authentic record of the presence of Jews in Frankfort comes to us in the account of a massacre of some hundred and eighty of them in 1241. This persecution was probably epidemic rather than indigenous in its nature, its germ distinctly traceable to those conscientious and comprehensive attempts of Louis the Saint, in the preceding year, to stamp out Judaism in his dominions. At any rate, for German Jews, an era of protection began under Frederick Barbarossa, and the Frankfort Jews among the rest, during the next hundred years, enjoyed the 'no history' which to the Jewish nation, pre-eminently amongst all others, must have been synonymous with happiness. But the story begins again about the middle of the fourteenth century when the Black Plague raged, and sanitary inspection, old style, took the form of declaring the wells to be poisoned, and of advising the burning and plunder of Jews by way of antidote. Jews were prolific, their hoards portable, their houses slightly built, so the burnings and the massacres and the liftings become intermittent and a little difficult to localise, till about the year 1430, when Frederick III.,

egged on by his clergy, made an order for
all Jews in Frankfort to reside out of sight
and sound of the holy Cathedral. A site just
without the ancient walls of the town, and
belonging to the council, was allotted to
them, and here, at their own expense, the
Jews built their *Judengasse*.

The street contained originally some hundred and ninety-six houses, and iron-sheeted
gates, kept fast closed on Sundays and saint
days, grew gradually to be barred from in-
side as well as outside on the Ghetto. The
pleasures and the hopes which Jews might
not share they came by slow degrees to hate
and to despise, and the men with the yellow
badges on their garments learnt to cringe
and stoop under their load, and the dark-eyed
women with the blue stripes to their veils
lifted them only to look upon their children.
Undeniably, by every outward test, the poor
pariahs of the Ghetto were degenerate, and
their sad and sordid lives must have looked
both repellent and unpicturesque to the
passer-by. But it may be doubted whether
the degeneracy went much deeper than the
costume. If the passer-by had passed in to
one of these gabled dwellings, when the de-
grading gaberdine and the disfiguring veil
were thrown aside, he would have come upon
an interior of home life which would have

struck him as strangely incongruous with the surroundings. Amid all the wretched physical squalor of the street he would have found little mental and less spiritual destitution. If the law of the land bid Jews shrink before men, the law of the Book bid them rejoice before God. Both laws they obeyed to the letter. Beating vainly at closed doors, they learnt to speak to the world with bated breath and whispered humbleness, but 'His courts' they entered, as it was commanded them, 'with thanksgiving,' and 'joyfully' sang hymns to Him. And the 'courts' came to be comprehensive of application, and the 'hymns' to include much literature. There was always a vivid domestic side to the religion of the Jews, and the alchemy of home life went far to turn the dross of the Ghetto into gold. Their Sabbath, in the picturesque phrase of their prayer-book, was 'a bride,' and her welcome, week by week, was of a right bridal sort. White cloths were spread and lamps lit in her honour. The shabbiest dwellings put on something of a festive air, and for 'Shobbus' the poorest haus-frau would manage to have ready at least one extra dish and several best and bright-coloured garments for her family. On the seventh day and on holy days the slouching pedlar and hawker fathers, with their packs cast off, were priests and teachers too, and every day the Ghetto children, for all their starved and stunted growth, had unlimited diet from the *Judengasse* stores of family affection and free schooling. They were probably, however, at no time very numerous, these Ghetto babies, for up to a quite comparatively recent date (1832) Jewish love-affairs were strictly under State control, and only fifteen couples a year were allowed to marry.

Ludwig Börne, or Löb Baruch as he is registered in the Frankfort synagogue (1786), was a result of one of these eagerly sought privileges, and it is easy to see how he came to write, ' Because I was born a slave I understand liberty; my birthplace was no longer than the *Judengasse,* and beyond its locked gates a foreign country began for me. Now, no town, no district, no province can content me. I can rest only with all Germany for my fatherland.' An eloquent expression enough of the repressed patriotism which was, perforce, inarticulate for centuries in the *Judengasse* of Frankfort.

Prison as the street must have seemed to its tenants, there was at least one occasion when its gates had the charms rather than the defects appertaining to bolts and bars. In 1498, a harassed, ragged little crowd from Nuremberg fled from their persecutors to

find in our Frankfort *Judengasse* a safe city
of refuge, and for a century or more the
Imperial coat-of-arms was gratefully em-
blazoned on the Ghetto gates as a sign to
the outer world that the Frankfort Jews,
though imprisoned, were protected. Yet we
may fairly doubt if the feeling of security
could have been much more than skin-deep,
since in 1711, when nearly the whole of the
street was burnt down, we find that some of
the poor souls were so afraid of insult and
plunder, that many refused to open their
doors to would-be rescuers, and so, to prevent
being pillaged, perished in the flames. An
oddly pathetic prose version of the famous
Ingoldsby martyr, who 'could stand dying,
but who couldn't stand pinching.'

When, in 1808, Napoleon made Frankfort
the capital of his new grand duchy, the Ghetto
gates were demolished, and many vexatious
restrictions were repealed. Such new hopes,
however, as the Frankfort Jews may have
begun to indulge, fell with Napoleon's down-
fall in 1815. Civil and political disabilities were
revived, and it was not till 1854 that the last
of these were erased from the statute-book.

The one house in that sad old street, the
stirring sermons in whose stones might be
'good in everything,' would be No. 148, the
little low-browed dwelling with the sign of

the Rose and Star—a veritable Rose of Dawn
it has proved—which was purchased more
than a hundred years ago [in 1780] by Meyer
Amschel Rothschild, the founder of the great
Rothschild house.   Every one knows the
fairy-like story of that old house; how Meyer
Amschel, intended by his parents to be a
rabbi, as many of his ancestors had been
before him, chose for himself a different way
of helping his fellow-men; how he went into
commerce, and made commerce, even in the
Ghetto, dignified and honourable, as he would
have made chimney-sweeping if he had
adopted it; how he became agent to the
Landgrave of Hesse-Cassel, how faithfully he
discharged his stewardship, and how his money
took to itself snowball properties, and changed
the tiny *Judengasse* tenement into gorgeous
mansions.   And the old stones would tell,
too, of how faithful were the old merchant
prince and the wife of his youth to early
associations; how sons and daughters grew up
and married, and moved to more aristocratic
neighbourhoods, but how Meyer Amschel and
his old wife clung to the shabby old home in
the Ghetto, and lived there all their lives, and
till she died, nearly fifty years ago.[1]   The very

---

[1] Gütle Rothschild, née Schnapper, died May 7, 1849.
Her eldest son, Amschel Meyer Rothschild, was born June
12, 1773, died December 6, 1855.

iron bars of those windows would speak if they could, saying never a word of their old bad uses, but telling only how kind and wrinkled hands were stretched out through them day by day, and year after year, dealing out bread to the hungry.   No. 148 could certainly tell the prettiest story in all the street, and preach the most suggestive line in all the sermons carted away with those stones of the Frankfort *Judengasse*.   And it would be a story with a sequel.   For when all the other sad old houses were demolished, the walls and rafters of No. 148 were carefully collected and numbered, and for a while reverently laid aside.   And now, re-erected, the house stands close by its old site, serving as the centre or depôt for the dispensing of the Rothschild charities in Frankfort.   Fanciful folks might almost be tempted to believe that stones with such experiences would be sufficiently sentient to rejoice at the pretty sentiment which refused to let them perish, and which, regarding them as relics, built them up afresh, and consecrated them to new and noble uses.

HEINRICH HEINE: A PLEA

'That blackguard Heine.'—CARLYLE.
' "Who was Heine?" A wicked man.'
                    CHARLES KINGSLEY.

THERE are some persons, some places, some things, which fall all too easily into ready-made definitions. Labels lie temptingly to hand, and specimens get duly docketed— 'rich as a Jew,' perhaps, or 'happy as a king' —with a promptitude and a precision which is not a trifle provoking to people of a nicely discriminative turn of mind. The amiable optimism which insists on an inseparable union between a Jew and his money, and discerns an alliterative link between kings and contentment, or makes now and again a monopoly of the virtues by labelling them 'Christian,' has, we suspect, a good deal to do with the manufacture of debatable definitions, and the ready fitting of slop-made judgments. Scores of such shallow platitudes occur to one's memory, some mischievous, some monotonous, some simply meaningless, and many of the most complacent have been tacked on to the telling of a life-story, brimful of contradictions, and running counter to most of the conventionalities. The story of one who was a Jew, and poor; a convert, without the zeal; a model of resignation, and yet no Christian; a poet, born under sternest conditions of prose, and with sad claims, by right of race, to the scorn of scorn and hate of hate, which we have been told is exclusively a poet's appanage —surely a story hardly susceptible of being summed up in an epithet. It is a life which has been told often, in many languages, and in much detail; this small sketch will glance only at such portions of it as seem to suggest the clue to a juster reading and a kindlier conclusion.

It was in the last month of the last year of the eighteenth century, in the little town of Düsseldorf in South Germany, that their eldest son Heinrich, or Harry as he seems to have been called in the family circle, was born unto Samson Heine, dealer in cloth, and Betty his wife. That eighteenth century had been but a dreary one for the Jews of Europe. It set in darkness on Heine's cradle, and on his 'mattress grave,' some fifty years later, the dawn of nineteenth century civilisation, for them, had scarcely broken. 'The heaviest burden that men can lay upon us,' wrote Spinoza, 'is not that they persecute us with

their hatred and scorn, but it is by the plant-
ing of hatred and scorn in our souls. That
is what does not let us breathe freely or see
clearly.' This subtlest effect of the poison
of persecution seemed to have entered the
Jewish system. Warned off from the high-
roads of life, and shunned for shambling along
its bye-paths, the banned and persecuted race,
looking out on the world from their ghettoes,
had grown to see most things in false perspec-
tive. Self loomed large on their blank horizon,
and gold shone more golden in the gloom.
God the Father, whose service demanded such
daily sacrifice, had lost something of that
divinest attribute; men, our brothers, could
the words have borne any but a 'tribal' sound?
Still, in those dim, dream-peopled ghettoes,
where visions of the absent, the distant, and
the past must have come to further perplex
and confuse the present, one actuality seems
to have been grasped among the shadows,
one ideal attained amid all the grim realities
of that most miserable time. Home life and
family affection had a sacredness for the worst
of these poor sordid Jews in a sense which,
to the best of those sottish little German potentates who so conscientiously despised them,
would have been unmeaning. Maidens were
honourably wed, and wives honoured and
children cherished in those wretched Juden-

strassen, where 'the houses look as if they could tell sorrowful stories,' after a fashion quite unknown at any, save the most exceptional, of the numerous coarse, corrupt, and ludicrously consequential little courts which were, at that period, representative of German culture.

The marriage of Heine's parents had been one of those faithful unions, under superficially unequal conditions, for which Jews seem to have a genius. It had been something of the old story, 'she was beautiful, and he fell in love'; she, pretty, piquant, cultivated, and the daughter of a physician of some local standing; he, just a respectable member of a respectable trading family, and ordinary all round, save for the distinction of one rich relative, a banker brother at Hamburg.

Betty's attractions, however, were all dangerous and undesirable possessions in the eyes of a prudent Jewish parent of the period, and Dr. von Geldern appears to have gladly given this charming daughter of his into the safe ownership of her somewhat commonplace wooer, whose chiefest faculty would seem to have been that of appreciation. It proved, nevertheless, a sufficiently happy marriage, and Betty herself, although possibly rather an acquiescent daughter than a responsive bride in the preliminaries, developed into a faithful wife and a most devoted mother, utilising her artistic tastes and her bright energy in the education of her children, and finding full satisfaction for her warm heart in their affection. Her eldest born was always passionately attached to her, and in the days of his youth, as in the years that so speedily 'drew nigh with no pleasure in them,' unto those latest of the 'evil days' when he lay so unconscionably long a-dying, and wrote long playful letters to her full of tender deceit, telling of health and wealth and friends, in place of pain and poverty and disease, through all that bitter, brilliant life of his, Heinrich Heine's relations with his mother were altogether beautiful, and go far to refute the criticism attributed, with I know not how much of truth, to Goethe, that 'the poet had every capacity save that for love!' 'In real love, as in perfect music,' says Bulwer Lytton in one of his novels, 'there must be a certain duration of time.' Heine's attachment to his mother was just lifelong; his first love he never forgot, nor, indeed, wholly forgave, and his devotion to his grisette wife not only preceded marriage, but survived it. Poor Heine! was it his genius or his race, or something of both, which conferred on him that fatal *pierre de touche* as regards reputation, '*il déplait invariablement à tous les imbeciles*' ?

In the very early boyhood of Heine some

light had broken in on the thick darkness, social and political, which enveloped Jewish fortunes. It was only a fitful gleam from the meteor-like course of the first Napoleon, but during those few years when, as Heine puts it, 'all boundaries were dislocated,' the Duchy of Berg, and its capital Düsseldorf, in common with more important states, were created French, and the Code Napoléon took the place for a while of that other, unwritten, code in which Jews were pariahs, to be condemned without evidence, and sentenced without appeal. Although the French occupation of Berg lasted unluckily but a few years (1806 till 1813), it did wonders in the way of individual civilisation, and Joachim Murat, during his governorship, seems really to have succeeded in introducing something of the 'sweet pineapple odour of politeness,' which Heine later notes as a characteristic of French manners, into the boorish, beerish little German principality. Although the time was all too short, and the conscription too universal for much national improvement to become evident, German burghers as well as German Jews had cause to rejoice in the change of rule. We hear of no 'noble' privileges, no licensed immunities nor immoralities during the term of the French occupation, and some healthier amusements than Jew-baiting were provided for the populace. With the departure of the French troops the clouds, which needed the storm of the '48 revolution to be effectually dispersed, gathered again. Still the foreign government, short as it was, had lasted long enough to make an impression for life on Heinrich Heine, and its most immediate effect was in the school influences it brought to bear upon him. Throughout all the States brought under French control, public education, by the Imperial edict of 1808, was settled on one broad system, and put under the general direction of the French Minister of Instruction. In accordance with this decree some suitable building in each selected district had to be utilised for class-rooms, the students had to be put into uniform, the teachers to be Frenchmen, and all subjects had to be taught through the medium of that language. The lycée at Düsseldorf was set up in an ancient Franciscan convent, and hither, at the age of ten, was Heine daily despatched. A bright little auburn-haired lad, full of fun and mischief, and mother-taught up to this date save for some small amount of Hebrew drilling which he seems to have received at the hands of a neighbouring Jewish instructor of youth, Harry had everything to learn, and discipline and the Latin declensions were among the first and greatest of his difficulties. Poet nature

and boy nature were both strong in him, and
it was so hard to sit droning out long dull lists
of words, which he was quite sure the origina-
tors of them had never had to do, for 'if the
Romans had had first to learn Latin,' he
ruminated, 'they never would have had time
to conquer the world'—so impossible he found
it to keep his eyes on the page, whilst the
very motes were dancing in the sunshine as it
poured in through the old convent window,
which was set just too high in the wall for
a safe jump into freedom.   One day the need
of sympathy, and possibly some unconscious
association from the dim old cloister, proved
momentarily too strong for the impressionable
little lad's Jewish instincts; he came across a
crucifix in some forgotten niche of the transformed convent; he looked up, he tells us, at
the roughly carved figure, and dropping on his
knees, prayed an earnest heterodox prayer,
'Oh, Thou poor once persecuted God, do help
me, if possible, to keep the irregular verbs in
my head!'

'Jewish instincts,' we said, and they could
have been scarcely more, for neither at home,
at school, nor in the streets was the atmosphere the boy breathed favourable to the
development of religious principles.   The
Judaism of that age was, superficially, very
much what the age had made of it; and its

followers and its persecutors alike combined
to render it mightly unattractive to susceptible natures. Samson Heine, stolid and
respectable, we may imagine doing his religious, as he did all his other duties and
avocations, in solemn routine fashion, laying
heavy honest hands on each prose detail, and
letting every bit of poetry slip through his fat
fingers, whilst his bright eager wife, with her
large ideas and her small vanities, ruled her
household, and read her Rousseau, and, feeling
the outer world shut from her by religion, and
the higher world barred from her by ritual,
found the whole thing cramping and unsatisfying to the last degree. 'Happy is he whom
his mother teacheth' runs an old Talmudic
proverb; but among the mother-taught lessons
of his childhood, the best was missing to
Heinrich Heine—the real difference between
'holy and profane' he never rightly learnt,
and thus it came to pass that Jewish instincts
—an ineradicable and an inalienable, but alas!
an incomplete inheritance of the sons of Israel
—were all that Judaism gave to this poet of
Jewish race.

One lingers over these early influences, the
right understanding of which goes far to
supply the key to some of the later puzzles.
Oddly enough, the clouds which by and by hid
the blue are discernible from the very first,

and these early years give the silver lining to those gathering clouds. In view of the dark days coming one at least rejoices that Heine's childhood was a happy one; at home the merry mischievous boy was quite a hero to his two younger brothers, and a hero and a companion both to his only sister, the Löttchen who was the occasion of his earliest recorded composition. It is a favourite recollection of this lady, who is living still,[1] how she, a blushing little maid of ten, won a good deal of unmerited praise for a school theme, till a trembling confession was extorted from her that the real author was her brother Harry. His mother, too, was exceedingly proud of her handsome eldest son, whose resemblance in many ways to her was the sweetest flattery. And besides the adoring home circle Harry found a great ally for playhours in an old French ex-drummer, who had marched to victory with Napoleon's legions, and who had plenty of tales to tell the boy of the wonderful invincible Kaiser, whom one day—blest never-to-be-forgotten vision—the boy actually saw ride through Düsseldorf on his famous white steed (1810). Heine never quite lost the glamour cast over him in his youth ; France, Germany, Judea, each in a sense his *patria,* was each, in the time to come, 'loved both ways,' each in turn

[1] Written in 1882.

mocked at bitterly enough when the mood
was on him, but always with France, the 'poet
of the nations' as our own English poetess
calls her, the sympathies of this cosmopolitan
poet were keenest—a perhaps not unnatural
state of feeling when we reflect how fact and
fiction both combined to produce it. The
French occupation of the principality had been
a veritable deliverance to its inhabitants,
Christian and Jewish alike, and what boy, in
his own person, led out of bondage, would not
have thrilled to such stories as the old drum-
mer had to tell of the real living hero of it
all? And the boy in question, we must bear
in mind, was a poet *in posse*.

In school, in spite of the difficulties of irregular verbs, Harry seems to have held his own,
and to have soon attracted the especial attention of the director. The chief selected for
the lycée at Düsseldorf had happened to be a
Roman Catholic abbé of decidedly Voltairian
views on most subjects, and attracted by the
boy and becoming acquainted with his family,
many a talk did Abbé Schallmayer have with
Frau Heine over the undoubted gifts and the
delightful imperfections of her son. It may
possibly have been altogether simple interest
in his bright young pupil, or perhaps Frau
Heine, pretty still, and charming always, was
herself an attraction to the schoolmaster, but

certain it is, whether a private taste for pretty women or a genuine pedagogic enthusiasm prompted his frequent calls, our abbé was a constant visitor at Samson Heine's, and Harry and Harry's future a never-failing theme for conversation. What was the boy to be? There was no room for much speculation if he were to remain a Jew—that path was narrow, if not straight, and admitted of small range of choice along its level line of commerce.

Betty, we know, was no staunch Jewess, and had her small personal ambitions to boot, so such opposition as there was to the abbé's plainly given counsel to make a Catholic of the boy, and give him his chance, came probably from the stolid, steady-going father, to whom custom spoke in echoes resonant enough to deaden the muffled tones of religion. No question, however, of sentiment or sacrifice was permitted to complicate, or elevate, the question; no sense of voluntary renunciation was suggested to the boy; no choice between the life and good, and the death and evil, between conscience and compromise, was presented to him. On the broadly comprehensive grounds that Judaism and trade had been good enough for the father, trade and Judaism must be good enough for the son—the matter was decided.

But still before the lad's prospects could be definitely settled, one important personage

remained to be consulted, the banker at
Hamburg, whose wealth had gained him
somewhat of the position of a family fetich.
What Uncle Solomon would say to a scheme
had no fictitious value about it; for even were
the oracle occasionally dumb, not seldom
would its speech be silver and its silence gold.
A rich uncle is a very solemn possession in an
impecunious family, so Harry, and Harry's
poetry, and Harry's powers generally, had to
be weighed in the Hamburg scales before any
standard value could be assigned to either
one of them.   For three years the balance
was held doubtful; the counting-house scales,
accurate as they usually were, could hardly
adjust themselves to the conditions of an unknown quantity, which 'young Heine' on an
office stool must certainly have proved to his
bewildered relatives.   One imagines him in
that correct and cramping atmosphere, fretting
as he had done in the old convent school-days
against its weary routine, longing with all the
half-understood strength of his poet nature for
the green hills and the mountain lakes, and
feeling absolutely stifled with all the solemn
interest shown over sordid matters.   He tells
us himself of some of his 'calculations' which
would wander far afield, and leave the figures
on the paper, to concern themselves with the
far more perplexing units which passed the

mirky office windows, as he complains, 'at the
same hour, with the same mien, making the
same motions, like the puppets in a town
house clock—reckoning, reckoning always on
the basis, twice two are four. Frightful should
it ever suddenly occur to one of these people
that twice two are properly five, and that he
therefore had miscalculated his whole life and
squandered it all away in a ghastly error!'
Many a poem too, sorrowful or fantastic, as the
mood took him, was scribbled in office hours,
and very probably on office paper, thence
to find a temporary home in the Hamburg
Watchman. What could be done with such a
lad? By every office standard he must inevitably have been found wanting, and one even
feels a sort of sympathy with the prosaic head
of the house who had made his money by the
exercise of such very different talents, and
whose notion of poetry corresponded very
nearly with Corporal Bunting's notion of love,
that it's by no means 'the great thing in life
boys and girls want to make it out to be—that
one does not eat it, nor drink it, and as for the
rest, why, it's bother.' It always was 'bother'
to the banker: all through his prosperous life
this poet nephew of his, who had the prophetic
impertinence to tell the old man once that he
owed him some gratitude for being born his
uncle, and for bearing his name, was an

unsatisfactory riddle.   Original genius of the
sort which could create a bank-book *ex nihilo*,
the millionaire could have appreciated, but
originality which ran into such unproductive
channels as poetry-book making was quite
beyond him, and that he never read the young
man's verses it is needless to say.   Even in
his own immediate family and for his first book
poor Harry found no audience, save his mother ;
and to the very end of his days Solomon Heine
for the life of him could see nothing in his
nephew but a *dumme Junge*, who never 'got
on,' and who made a jest of most things, even
of his wealthy and respectable relatives.

It was scarcely the old man's fault ; one can
only see to the limits of one's vision, and a
poet's soul was not well within Solomon Heine's
range.   According to his lights he was not
ungenerous.   That Harry had not the making
of a clerk in him, those three probationary
years had proved to demonstration, and in the
determination at which the banker presently
arrived, of giving those indefinite talents which
he only understood enough to doubt, a chance
of development by paying for a three years'
university course at Bonn, he seems to have
come fully up to any reasonable ideal of a rich
uncle.   It is just possible that a secondary
motive influenced his generosity, for Harry,
besides scribbling, had found a relief from

office work by falling in love with one of the
banker's daughters, who would seem not to
have shared the family distaste for poetry.
The little idyl was of course out of the question
in so realistic a circle, and the young lady, to
do her justice, seems herself to have been
speedily reconverted to the proper principles
in which she had been trained. No unfit
pendant to the 'Amy, shallow-hearted' with
whom a more recent generation is more
familiar, this Cousin Amy of poor Heine's
married and 'kept her carriage' with all due
despatch, whilst he, at college, was essaying to
mend his 'heart broken in two' with all the
styptics which are as old and, alas, as hurtful
as such fractures. Poetical exaggeration notwithstanding—and besides her own especial
love-elegy, Amalie Heine, under thin disguises,
is the heroine of very many of the love-poems
—there is little room for doubt, that if not so
seriously injured as he thought, Heine's heart
did nevertheless receive a wound, which ached
for many and many a long day, from this girl's
weak or wilful inconstancy. Heartache is,
however, nearly as much a matter-of-course
episode in most young people's lives as measles,
and the consequences of either malady are
only very exceptionally serious.

Heine's youthful disappointment is of chief
interest as having indirectly led to what was

really the determining event of his life. When Amalie's parents shrewdly determined on separation as the best course to be pursued with the cousins, and the university plan had been accepted by Harry, his future, which was to date from degree-taking, came on for discussion. Except in an 'other-worldly' sense there was, in truth, but a very limited 'future' possible to Jews of talent. The only open profession was that of medicine, and for that, like the son of Moses Mendelssohn, young Heine had a positive distaste. Commerce, that first and final resource of the race, which had had to satisfy Joseph Mendelssohn, like a good many others equally ill-fitted for it, was not possible to Heine, for he had sufficiently shown, not only dislike, but positive incapacity for business routine. The law suggested itself, as affording an excellent arena for those ready powers of argument and repartee which in the family circle were occasionally embarrassing, and the profession of an advocate, with the vague 'opportunities' it included, when pressed upon young Heine, was not unalluring to him. The immediate future was probably what most occupied his thoughts; the freedom of a university life, the flowing river in place of those bustling streets, shelves full of books exchanged for those dreary office ledgers, youthful comrades in the stead of solemnly irritated old clerks.   Whether the fact that conversion was a condition of most of the delights, an inevitable preliminary of all the benefits of that visionary future; whether the grim truth that 'a certificate of baptism was a necessary card of admission to European culture,' was openly debated and defended, or silently and shamefacedly slurred over in these family councils, does not appear.   No record remains to us but the fact that the young student successfully passed his examination in May, 1825; that he was admitted to his degree on July 20, and that between these two dates—to be precise, on the 28th of June—he was baptized as a Protestant with two clergymen for his sponsors. 'Lest I be poor and deny thee' was Agur's prayer, and a wise one; for shivering Poverty, clutching at the drapery of Desire, makes unto herself many a fine, mean, flimsy garment. With no gleam of conviction to cast a flickering halo of enthusiasm over the act, and with no shadow of overwhelming circumstance to somewhat veil it, Heine made his deliberate surrender of conscience to expediency.   It was full-grown apostasy, neither conscientious conversion, nor childish drifting into another faith.   'No man's soul is alone,' Ruskin tells us in his uncompromising way, 'Laocoon or Tobit, the serpent has it by the heart or the angel by the hand.'   For the rest of his life

Heine was in the grip of the serpent, and that, it seems to us, was the secret of his perpetual unrest. Maimed lives are common enough; blind or deaf, or minus a leg or an arm, or plus innumerable bruises, one yet goes on living, and with the help of time and philosophy sorrow of most sorts grows bearable. Hearts are tough; but the soul is more sensitive to injuries, is, to many of us, the veritable, vulnerable *tendo Achillis* on which our mothers lay their tender, detaining, unavailing hands. Heine sold his soul, and that he never received the price must have perpetually renewed the memory of the bargain. He, one of the 'body-guards of Jehovah,' had suffered himself to be bribed from his post. He never lost his sickening sense of that humiliation; it may be read between the lines, alike of the most brilliant of his prose, of the most tender of his poems, of the most mocking of his often quoted jests.

> 'They have told thee a-many stories,
>   And much complaint have made;
> And yet my heart's true anguish
>   That never have they said.
>
> 'They shook their heads protesting,
>   They made a great to-do;
> They called me a wicked fellow,
>   And thou believedst it true.

> 'And yet the worst of all things,
>   Of that they were not aware,
> The darkest and the saddest,
>   That in my heart I bear.' [1]

And it was a burden he never laid down; it embittered his relationships and jeopardised his friendships, and set him at variance with himself. 'I get up in the night and look in the glass and curse myself,' we find him writing to one of his old Jewish fellow-workers in the New Jerusalem movement (Moser), or checking himself in the course of a violent tirade against converts, in which Börne had joined, to bitterly exclaim, 'It is ill talking of ropes in the house of one who has been hanged.' Wherever he treats of Jewish subjects, and the theme seems always to have had for him the fascination which is said to tempt sinners to revisit the scene of their sins, we seem to read remorse between the melodious, mocking lines. Now it is Moses Lump who is laughed at in half tones of envy for his ignorant, unbarterable belief in the virtue of unsnuffed candles; now it is Jehudah Halevi, whose love for the mistress, the *Herzensdame*, 'whose name was Jerusalem,' is sung with a sympathy and an intensity impossible to one who had not felt a like passion, and was not

---

[1] The translation is by the late Amy Levy.

bitterly conscious of having forfeited the right
to avow it.   The sense of his moral mercenary
suicide, in truth, rarely left him.   His nature
was too conscientious for the strain thus set
upon it; his 'wickedness' and 'blackguardism,'
such as they were, were often but passionate
efforts to throw his old man of the sea, his
heavy burden of self-reproach; and his jests
sound not unseldom as so many untranslatable
cries.   He had bargained away his birthright
for the hope of a mess of pottage, and the evil
taste of the base contract clung to the poor
paralysed lips when 'even kissing had no effect
upon them.'   And but a thin, unsatisfying,
and terribly intermittent 'mess,' too, it proved,
and the share in it which his uncle, and his
uncle's heirs, provided was very bitter in the
eating.   The story of his struggles, are they
not written in the chronicles of the im-
mortals? and his 'monument,' is it not
standing yet 'in the new stone premises of
his publishers?'[1]

His biographers—his niece, the Princessa
della Rocca, among the latest—have made
every incident of Heine's life as familiar as
his own books have made his genius to English
readers, and Mr. Stigand, following Herr

---

[1] Messrs. Campe and Hoffmann erected their new offices
during the publication (not too well paid) of the poet's
works.

Strodtman, has given us an exhaustive record
of the poet's life at home and in exile; in
the Germany which was so harsh and in the
France which was so tender with him; with
the respectable German relatives, who read
his books at last and were none the wiser, and
with the unlettered French wife, who could
not read a single word of them all, and who
yet understood her poet by virtue of the love
which passeth understanding, and was in this
case entirely independent of it.   This sketch
trenches on no such well-filled ground; it
presumes to touch only on the fault which
gave to life and genius both that odd pathetic
twist, and to glance at the suffering, which, if
there be any saving power in anguish, might
surely be held by the most self-righteous as
some atonement for the 'blackguardism.'

> 'Oh ! not little when pain
> Is most quelling, and man
> Easily quelled, and the fine
> Temper of genius so soon
> Thrills at each smart, is the praise
> Not to have yielded to pain.'[1]

Seven years on the rack is no small test
of the heroic temperament; to lie sick and
solitary, stretched on a 'mattress grave,' the
back bent and twisted, the legs paralysed, the

[1] Matthew Arnold, *Heinrich Heine.*

hands powerless, and with the senses of sight
and taste fast failing.   At any time within
that seven years Heine might well have gained
the gold medal in capability of suffering for
which, in his whimsical way, he talked of com-
peting, should such a prize be offered at the
Paris Exhibition.[1]   And the long days, with
'no pleasure in them,' were so drearily many ;
the silver cord was so slowly loosed, the
golden bowl seemed broken on the wheel.
His very friends grew tired.   'One must love
one's friends with all their failings, but it is a
great failing to be ill,' says Madame Sevigné,
and, as the years went by, more and more
deserted grew the sick-chamber.   He never
complained ; his sweet, ungrudging nature
found excuses for desertion and content in
loneliness, in the reflection that he was in
truth 'unconscionably long a-dying.'   'Never
have I seen,' says Lady Duff-Gordon, in her
Recollections of Heine, and she herself was no
mean exemplar of bravely-borne pain, 'never
have I seen a man bear such horrible pain and
misery in so perfectly unaffected a manner.
He neither paraded his anguish, nor tried to
conceal it, or to put on any stoical airs.   He
was pleased to see tears in my eyes, and then
at once set to work to make me laugh heartily,
which pleased him just as much.'

[1] The Exhibition of 1855.

'Don't tell my wife,' he exclaims one day,
when a paroxysm that should have been fatal
was not, and the doctor expressed what he
meant for a reassuring belief, that it would
not hasten the end. 'Don't tell my wife '—
we seem to hear that sad little jest, so infinitely
sadder than a moan, and our own eyes moisten.
Perfectly upright geniuses, when suffering from
dyspepsia, have not always shown as much
consideration for their perfectly proper wives
as does this 'blackguard' Heine, under torture,
for his. It is conceivable that under exceptional circumstances a man may contrive to
be a hero to his valet, but, unless he be truly
heroic, he will not be able to keep up the
character to his wife. Heine managed both.
Madame Heine is still living,[1] and one may
not say much of a love that was truly strong
as death, and that the many waters of affliction
could not quench. But the valet test, we may
hint, was fulfilled ; for the old servant who
helped to tend him in that terrible illness
lives still with Madame Heine, and cries 'for
company' when the widow's talk falls, as it
falls often, on the days of her youth and her
'*pauvre Henri.*' There are traditional records
in plenty of his cheerful courage, his patient
unselfishness, his unfailing endurance of well-
nigh unendurable pain. ' *Dieu me pardonnera,*

[1] Written in 1882.

c'est son métier,' the dying lips part to say, still with that sweet, inseparable smile playing about them.   Shall man be more just than God?   Shall we leave to Him for ever the monopoly of His *métier?*

DANIEL DERONDA AND HIS
JEWISH CRITICS

George Eliot and Judaism. An attempt to appreciate *Daniel Deronda.* By Professor DAVID
KAUFMANN, of the Jewish Theological Seminary, Buda-Pesth. Translated from the German
by J. W. FERRIER, 1877. Edinburgh and
London : William Blackwood and Sons.

THE latest echo from the critical chorus which
has greeted *Daniel Deronda* comes to us
from Germany, in the form of a small book
by Dr. Kaufmann, professor in the recently
instituted Jewish Theological Seminary at
Buda-Pesth. A certain prominence, which
its very excellent translation into English
confers upon this work, seems to be due less
to any special or novel feature in its criticism
than to the larger purpose shadowed forth
in the title, 'George Eliot and Judaism.'
It is advowedly 'an attempt to appreciate
Daniel Deronda,' and is valuable and interesting to English society not as a critique
on the plot or the characters of the book—

on which points it strikes us, in more than one instance, as somewhat weak and one-sided—but as indicating from a Jewish standpoint in how far and how truly modern Judaism is therein represented. Unappreciative as the great mass of the reading public have shown themselves to the latest of George Eliot's novels, the work has excited a considerable amount of curiosity and admiration on the ground of the intimate knowledge its author has evinced of the inner lives and of the little-read literature of the 'Great Unknown of humanity.' We think Dr. Kaufmann goes too far when he says, 'The majority of readers view the world to which they are introduced in *Daniel Deronda* as one foreign, strange, and repulsive. . . . It is not only the Jew of flesh and blood whom men encounter every day upon the streets that they hate, but the Jew under whatever shape he may appear, and even the airy productions of the poet's fancy are denounced when they venture to take that people as their subject' (p. 92). We think this view concedes very much too much to prejudice; but it is undoubtedly a fact that the first serious attempt by a great writer to make Jews and Judaism the central interest of a great work, has produced a certain sense of discord on the public ear, and that criticism has for the most part

run in the minor key. Mr. Swinburne, perhaps, strikes the most distinctly jarring chord,
when, in his lately published 'Note on
Charlotte Brontë,' he owns to possessing 'no
ear for the melodies of a Jew's harp,' and,
disclaiming 'a taste for the dissection of
dolls,' 'leaves Daniel Deronda to his natural
place over the rag-shop door' (pp. 21, 22).
Even an ear so politely and elegantly owned
defective might be able, it could be imagined,
to catch an echo from the 'choir invisible';
and poetic insight, one might almost venture
to think, should be able to discern in poetic
aspirations, however unfamiliar and even
alien to itself, something different from bran.
This arrow is too heavily tipped to fly straight
to the goal. There are numbers, however,
of the like school who, with more excuse
than Mr. Algernon Swinburne, fail to 'see
anything' in *Daniel Deronda*, and a criticism we once overheard in the Louvre occurs
to us as pertinent to this point. The picture
was Correggio's 'Marriage of St. Katharine,'
and to an Englishman standing near us it
evidently did not fulfil preconceived conceptions of a marriage ceremony. He looked at
it long, and at last turned disappointed away,
audibly muttering, 'Well, I can't see anything in it.' That was evident, but the
failure was not in the picture. Preconceived

conceptions count for much, whether the artist be a Correggio or a George Eliot, and ignorance and prejudice are ill-fitting spectacles wherewith to assist vision.

If it be an axiom that a man should be judged by his peers, we should think that George Eliot would herself prefer that her work should be weighed in the balance by those qualified to hold the scales, and should by them, if at all, be pronounced 'wanting.' A book of which Judaism is the acknowledged theme should appeal to Jews for judgment, and thus the question becomes an interesting one to the outer world,—What do the Jews themselves think of *Daniel Deronda*? Are the aspirations of Mordecai regarded by them as the expression of a poet's dream, or a nation's hope? What, in short, is the aspect of modern Judaism to the book?

'Modern' Judaism is itself, perhaps, a convenient rather than a correct figure of speech. There are modern manners to which modern Jews necessarily conform, and which have a tendency to tone down the outward and special characteristics of Judaism, as of everything else, to a general socially-undistinguishable level. But men are not necessarily dumb because they do not speak much or loudly of such very personal matters as their religious hopes and beliefs, more especially if in these days they are so little in the fashion as to hold strong convictions on such subjects. Our author distinctly formulates the opinion that 'men may give all due allegiance to a foreign State without ceasing to belong to their own people' (p. 21); and in the same sense as we may conceive a man honestly fulfilling all dues as good husband and good father to his living and lawful wife and children, and yet holding tenderly in the unguessed-at depths of memory some long-ago-lost love, so is it conceivable of many an unromantic-looking nineteenth century Jew, who soberly performs all good citizen duties, that the unspoken name of Jerusalem is still enshrined in like unguessed-at depths, as the 'perfection of beauty,' 'the joy of the whole earth.' Conventionalities conduce to silence on such topics, and therefore it is to published rather than to spoken Jewish criticisms we must turn in our inquiry, and the little book under review certainly helps us to a definite answer.

And we may notice, as a significant fact, that while on the part of general critics there has been some differing even in their adverse judgments, and a more than partial failure to grasp the idea of the book, there seems both here and abroad a grateful consensus of Jewish opinion that not only has George Eliot truly depicted the externals of

Jewish *life,* which was a comparatively easy
task, but has also correctly represented
Jewish thought and the ideas underlying
Judaism. Our author emphatically says,
'*Daniel Deronda* is a Jewish book, not
only in the sense that it treats of Jews, but
also in the sense that it is pre-eminently
fitted for being understood and appreciated
by Jews' (p. 90); and again, 'it will always
be gratefully declared,' he concludes, '*that
George Eliot has deserved right well of Judaism*'
(p. 95).   Does this, then, mean that the
'national' idea is a rooted, practical hope?
Do English Jews, undistinguishable in the
mass from other Englishmen, really and truly
hold the desire, like Mordecai, of 'founding
a new Jewish polity, grand, simple, just, like
the old'? (*Daniel Deronda,* Book iv.)   Do
they indeed design to devote their 'wealth
to redeem the soil from debauched and
paupered conquerors,' to cleanse their fair
land from 'the hideous obloquy of Christian
strife, which the Turk gazes at as at the fight-
ing of wild beasts to which he has lent an
arena' (*ibidem*)?   Was Daniel's honeymoon-
mission to the East to have this practical
result?   The general Jewish verdict, as we
read it, scarcely concedes so much; it sees
rather in the closing scene of *Daniel Deronda*
the only weak spot in the book.   Vague and

visionary as are all honeymoon anticipations, those of Daniel, their beauty and unselfishness notwithstanding, strike Jewish readers as even more unsubstantial, even less likely of realisation, than such imaginings in general. Possibly, as in the old days of the Babylonian exile, 'there be some that dream' of an actual restoration, of a Palestine which should be the Switzerland of Asia Minor, which, crowned with ancient laurels, might sit enthroned in piece and plenty,—

'Dispensing harvest, sowing the To-Be.'

But save with such few and faithful dreamers, memory scarcely blossoms into hope, and hope most certainly has not yet ripened into strong desire. It may come; but at present we apprehend the majority of Jews see the 'future of Judaism' not in the form of a centralised and localised nationality, but rather in the destiny foreshadowed by our author, in which 'Israel will be greatest when she labours under every zone,' when 'her children shall have spread themselves abroad, bearing the ineradicable seeds of eternal truth' (pp. 86, 87). This conception of 'nationality' would point rather to a spiritual than to a temporal sovereignty, to a supremacy of mind rather than of matter, and appears to be in accord with the tone pervading both ancient and modern Jewish literature, which exhibits Judaism as a perpetual living force, maintained from within rather than from without, and destined continually to influence religious thought, and to survive all dispensations.

In his undefined mission to the East Deronda is, therefore, to that extent perhaps, out of harmony with the general tone of modern Jewish thought. We at least are constrained to think that more Jews of the present day would be ready to follow Mordecai in imagination than Deronda in person to Judæa. It is, nevertheless, in strict artistic unity that, shut out for five-and-twenty years from actual practical knowledge of his people, Deronda should represent the *ideal* rather than the *idea* of Judaism. Mordecai, sketched as he is supposed to be from the life, with his deep poetic yearnings, which are stayed on the threshold of action, strikes us as a truer and more typical figure than Deronda hastening to their fulfilment. And on the subject of these same vague yearnings another point suggests itself. We have heard it said that the religious belief of Mordecai centres rather in the destiny of his race than in the Being who has appointed that destiny, and we have heard it questioned whether the theism of Mordecai is sufficiently defined to be fairly

representative of Jewish thought, or if Judaism
indeed is also passing under that wave of
Pantheism which, like the waters of old, is
threatening to submerge all ancient land-
marks, and to leave visible only 'the tops of
the mountains' of revealed religion. This
seems a criticism based rather on negative
than on positive evidence, and derived possibly
from the obvious leanings of George Eliot's
other writings, and it is, perhaps, somewhat
unfair to assume that, even if, on this point,
she does not sympathise with the Jews, she
has any intention of colouring her picture of
modern Judaism with intellectual prepossess-
sions of her own. In the silence of Mordecai
with respect to his beliefs, he represents the
great body of Jews, whose religion finds
expression rather in action than in formula,
and who are slow to indulge in theological
speculations. Mordecai was true to Jewish
characteristics in the fact that his belief was
concealed beneath his hopes and aspirations,
but had he in any degree shared the views
of the new school of sceptics, he could not
have been the typical Jew, who sees in the
unity of his people a symbol of the unity of
his God.

The pure theism of Judaism may be said
to have its poles in the anthropomorphic
utterances of some of the Rabbinical writers,

E

and in the present pantheism of the extreme
German school; but we should say that the
ordinary, the representative Jewish thought
of the day lies between these two extremes,
and, in so far as it gives expression to any
belief on the subject, distinctly recognises
a personal God presiding over human destiny
and natural laws. There may be here and
there an inquiring spirit that wanders so far
afield that his attraction towards his people
is lost, and with it the influence his genius
should exert; but Jewish thought, if owning
a somewhat nebulous conception of the Deity,
slowly progressing towards one fuller and
grander, cannot be said to be drifting towards
Pantheism. Judaism, unlike many other faiths,
has not a history and a religious belief apart,—
the one not only includes and supplements,
but is actually non-existent, 'unthinkable,'
without the other. Thus to have made an
earnest Jew, with the strong racial instinct of
Mordecai, a weak theist, would have been an
inartistic conception, and Jewish criticism has
not discovered this flaw in George Eliot's
exceptional but faithful Jewish portraiture.
Judging, then, from such sources as are open
to us, we are led to infer that the feeling
of nationality is still deeply rooted in the
Jewish race, and that the religious feeling
from which it is inseparable perhaps gives it

the strength and depth to exist and to continue to exist without the external props of 'a local habitation and a name.' Dr. Kaufmann, therefore, very well expresses what appears to be the general conviction of his co-religionists, when he suggests that 'in the very circumstance of dispersion may lie fulfilment' (p. 87).

MANASSEH BEN ISRAEL

PRINTER AND PATRIOT

WHEN the prophet of the Hebrews, some six-and-twenty hundred years ago, thundered forth his stirring 'Go through! go through the gates! prepare a way, lift up a standard for the people!' it may, without irreverence, be doubted if he foresaw how literally his charge would be fulfilled by one of his own race in the seventeenth century of the Christian era. The story of how it was done may perhaps be worth retelling, since many subjects of lesser moment have found more chroniclers.

It was in 1290 that gates, which in England had long been ominously creaking on their hinges, were deliberately swung-to, and bolted and barred by Church and State on the unhappy Jews, who on that bleak November day stood shivering along the coast. 'Thy waves and thy billows have passed over me' must have lost in tender allegory and gained some added force of literalness that wintry afternoon. Scarce any of the

descendants of that exodus can have had
share in the return. Of such of the refugees
as reached the opposite ports few found foothold, and fewer still asylum. The most, and
perhaps they were the most fortunate of the
fifteen thousand, were quick in gaining foreign
graves. Those who made for the nearest
neighbouring shores of France, forgetful, or
perhaps ignorant, of the recent experiences of
their French brethren under Philip Augustus,
lived on to earn a like knowledge for themselves, and to undergo, a few years later,
another expulsion under Philip the Fair.
Those who went farther fared worse, for over
the German States the Imperial eagle of
Rome no longer brooded, now to protect and
now to prey on its victims; the struggle
between the free cities and the multitudinous
petty princelings was working to its climax,
and whether at bitter strife, or whether
pausing for a brief while to recruit their
powers, landgrave and burgher, on one subject,
were always of one mind. To plunder at need
or to persecute at leisure, Jews were held to
be handy and fair game for either side.

Far northward or far southward that ragged
English mob were hardly fit to travel. Some
remnant, perhaps, made effort to reach the
semi-barbarous settlements in Russia and
Poland, but few can have been sanguine

enough to set out for distant Spain in hope of
a welcome but rarely accorded to such very
poor relations. And even in the Peninsula
the security which Jews had hitherto experi-
enced had by this date received several severe
shocks. Two centuries later and the tide of
civilisation had rolled definitely and drearily
back on the soil which Jews had largely helped
to cultivate, and left it bare, and yet a little
longer, Portugal, become a province of Spain,
had followed the cruel fashions of its suzerain.

By the close of the sixteenth century a
settlement of the dispossessed Spanish and
Portuguese Jews had been formed in Holland,
and Amsterdam was growing into a strange
Dutch likeness of a new Jerusalem, for Holland alone among the nations at this period
gave a welcome to all citizens in the spirit of
Virgil's famous line, ' *Tros Rutulusve fuat, nullo
discrimine habebo.*' And the refugees, who at
this date claimed the hospitality of the States,
were of a sort to make the Dutch in love with
their own unfashionable virtue of religious
tolerance. Under Moorish sway, for centuries,
commerce had been but one of the pursuits
open to the Jews and followed by the Jews
of the Peninsula, and thus it was a crowd, not
of financiers and traders only or chiefly, but
of cultivated scholars, physicians, statesmen,
and land-owners, whom Catholic bigotry had

exiled. The thin disguise of new Christians was soon thrown off by these Jews, and they became to real Christians, to such men as Vossius and Caspar Barlæus, who welcomed them and made friends of them, a revelation of Judaism.

It was after the great *auto-da-fé* of January 1605, that Joseph ben Israel, with a host of other Jews, broken in health and broken in fortune, left the land which bigotry and persecution had made hideous to them, and joined the peaceful and prosperous settlement in Amsterdam. The youngest of Ben Israel's transplanted family was the year-old Manasseh, who had been born in Lisbon a few months before their flight. He seems to have been from the first a promising and intelligent lad, and his tutor, one Isaac Uziel, who was a minister of the congregation, and a somewhat famous mathematician and physician to boot, formed a high opinion of the boy's abilities. He did not, however, live to see them verified; when Manasseh was but eighteen the Rabbi died, and his clever pupil was thought worthy to be appointed to the vacated office. It was an honoured and an honourable, but scarcely a lucrative, post to which Manasseh thus succeeded, and the problem of living soon became further complicated by an early marriage and a young family. Manasseh had to cast about him for supplementary means of support, and

he presently found it in the establishment of
a printing press.   Whether the type gave
impetus to the pen, or whether the pen had
inspired the idea of the press, is hard to decide;
but it is, at least, certain that before he was
twenty-five, Manasseh had found congenial
work and plenty of it.   He taught and he
preached, and both in the school-room and in
the pulpit he was useful and effective, but it
was in his library that he felt really happy
and at home.   Manasseh was a born scholar
and an omnivorous reader, bound to develop
into a prolific, if not a profound, writer.   The
work which first established his fame bears
traces of this, and is, in point of fact, less of
a composition than a compilation.   The first
part of this book, *The Conciliator,* was published in 1632, after five years' labour had been
expended on it, and it is computed to contain
quotations from, or references to, over 200
Hebrew, and 50 Latin and Greek authors.
Its object was to harmonise (*conciliador*) conflicting passages in the Pentateuch, and it was
written in Spanish, although it could have
been composed with equal facility in any one
of half-a-dozen other languages, for Manasseh
was a most accomplished linguist.

Although not the first book which was
issued from his press, for a completely edited
prayer-book and a Hebrew grammar had been

published in 1627, *The Conciliator* was the first
work that attracted the attention of the
learned world to the Amsterdam Rabbi.
Manasseh had the advantage of literary con-
nections of his own, through his wife, who was
a great-granddaughter of Abarbanel — that
same Isaac Abarbanel, the scholar and patriot,
who in 1490 headed the deputation to Ferdi-
nand and Isabella, which was so dramatically
cut short by Torquemada.

Like *The Conciliator*, all Manasseh's subsequent literary ventures met with ready appreciation, but with more appreciation, it would
seem, than solid result, for his means appear
to have been always insufficient for his modest
wants, and in 1640 we find him seriously con-
templating emigration to Brazil on a trading
venture. Two members of his congregation,
which, as a body, does not seem to have acted
liberally towards him, came forward, however,
at this crisis in his affairs, and conferred a
benefit all round by establishing a college and
appointing Manasseh the principal, with an
adequate salary. This ready use of some portion of their wealth has made the brothers
Pereira more distinguished than for its possession. Still, it must not be inferred that Manasseh had been, up to this date, a friendless,
if a somewhat impecunious, student, only that,
as is rather perhaps the wont of poor prophets

in their own country, his admirers had had to
come from the outer before they reached the
inner circle. He had certainly achieved a
European celebrity in the Republic of letters
before his friends at Amsterdam had discovered
much more than the fact that he printed very
superior prayer-books. He had won over,
amongst others, the prejudiced author of the
Law of Nations, to own him, a Jew, for a
familiar friend, before some of the wealthier
heads of his own congregation had claimed a
like privilege; and Grotius, then Swedish am-
bassador at Paris, was actually writing to him,
and proffering friendly services, at the very
time that the Amsterdam congregation were
calmly receiving his enforced farewells. There
was something, perhaps, of irony in the situa
tion, but Manasseh, like Maimonides, had no
littleness of disposition, no inflammable self-
love quick to take fire; he loved his people
truly enough to understand them and to make
allowances, had even, perhaps, some humorous
perception of the national obtuseness to native
talent when unarrayed in purple and fine linen,
or until duly recognised by the wearers of
such.

Set free, by the liberality of Abraham and
Isaac Pereira, from the pressure of everyday
cares, Manasseh again devoted himself to his
books, and turned out a succession of treatises.

History, Philosophy, Theology, he attacked
them all in turn, and there is, perhaps, something besides rapidity of execution which suggests an idea of manufacture in most of these
works. A treatise which he published about
1650, and which attracted very wide notice,
significantly illustrated his rather fatal facility
for ready writing. The treatise was entitled
The Hope of Israel, and sought to prove no
less than that some aborigines in America,
whose very existence was doubtful, were lineal
descendants of the lost ten tribes. The Hope
itself seems to have rested on no more solid
foundation than a traveller's tale of savages
met with in the wilds, who included something
that sounded like the שמע (Shemang [1]) in their
vernacular. The story was quickly translated
into several languages, but it was almost as
quickly disproved, and Manasseh's deductions
from it were subsequently rather roughly
criticised. Truth to say, the accumulated
stores of his mind were ground down and
sifted and sown broadcast in somewhat careless
and indigestible masses, and their general
character gives an uncomfortable impression
of machine-work rather than of hand-work.
And the proportion of what he wrote was as
nothing compared to what he contemplated
writing. Perhaps those never-written books of

---

[1] Short declaration of belief in Unity (Deut. vi. 4).

his would have proved the most readable; he might have shown us himself, his wise, tolerant, enthusiastic self, in them. But instead, we possess, in his shelves on shelves of published compilations of dead men's minds, only duly labelled and catalogued selections from learned mummies.

The dream of Manasseh was to compose a 'Heroic History,' a significant title which shadows forth the worthy record he would have delighted in compiling from Jewish annals. It is as well, perhaps, that the title is all we have of the work, for he was too good an idealist to prove a good historian. He cared too much, and he knew too much, to write a reliable or a readable history of his people. To him, as to many of us, Robert Browning's words might be applied—

'So you saw yourself as you wished you were—
  As you might have been, as you cannot be—
Earth here rebuked by Olympus there,
  And grew content in your poor degree.'[1]

He, at any rate, had good reason to grow content in his degree, for he was destined to make an epoch in the 'Heroic History,' instead of being, as he 'wished he were,' the reciter, and probably the prosy reciter, of several. Certain it is that, great scholar,

[1] 'Old Pictures from Florence.'

successful preacher, and voluminous writer as
was Manasseh ben Israel, it was not till he
was fifty years old that he found his real
vocation.   He had felt at it for years, his
books were more or less blind gropings after
it, his friendships with the eminent and highly
placed personages of his time were all unconscious means to a conscious end, and his very
character was a factor in his gradually formed
purpose.   His whole life had been an up-
holding of the 'standard'; publicists who
sneered at the ostentatious rich Jew, priests
who railed at the degraded poor Jew, were
each bound to recognise in Manasseh ben Israel
a Jew of another type: one poor yet self-
respecting, sought after yet unostentatious,
conservative yet cosmopolitan, learned yet
undogmatic.   They might question if this
Amsterdam Rabbi were *sui generis*, but they
were at least willing to find out if he were in
essentials what he claimed to be, fairly representative of the fairly treated members of
his race.   So the 'way was prepared' by the
'standard' being raised.   Which, of the many
long-closed 'gates,' was to open for the people
to pass through ?

Manasseh looked around on Europe.   He
sought a safe and secure resting-place for the
tribe of wandering foot and weary heart, where,
no longer weary and wandering, they might

cease to be 'tribal.' He sought a place where 'protection' should not be given as a sordid bribe, nor conferred as a fickle favour, but claimed as an inalienable right, and shared in common with all law-abiding citizens. His thoughts turned for a while on Sweden, and there was some correspondence to that end with the young Queen Christina, but this failing, or falling through, his hopes were almost at once definitely directed towards England. It was a wise selection and a happy one, and the course of events, and the time and the temper of the people, seemed all upon his side. The faithless Stuart king had but lately expiated his hateful, harmful weakness on the scaffold, and sentiment was far as yet from setting the nimbus of saint and martyr on that handsome, treacherous head. The echoes of John Hampden's brave voice seemed still vibrating in the air, and Englishmen, but freshly reminded of their rights, were growing keen and eager in the scenting out of wrongs; quick to discover, and fierce to redress evils which had long lain rooted and rotting, and unheeded. The pompous *insouciance* of the first Stuart king, the frivolous *insouciance* of the second, were now being resented in inevitable reaction. The court no longer led the fashion; the people had come to the front and were growing grimly, even grotesquely, in earnest. The very fashion of speaking seems to have changed with the new need for strong, terse expression. Men greeted each other with old-fashioned Bible greetings; they named their children after those 'great ones gone,' or with even quainter effect in some simple selected Bible phrase; the very tones of the Prophets seemed to resound in White-hall, and Englishmen to have become, in a wide, unsensational sense, not men only of the sword, or of the plough, but men of the Book, and that Book the Bible. Liberty of conscience, equality before the law for all religious denominations, had been the un-conditional demand of that wonderful army of Independents, and although the Catholics were the immediate cause and object of this appeal, yet Manasseh, watching events from the calm standpoint of a keenly interested onlooker, thought he discerned in the listen-ing attitude of the English Parliament, a favourable omen of the attention he desired to claim for his clients, since it was not alone for political, but for religious, rights that he meant to plead.

He did not, however, actually come to England till 1655, when the way for personal intercession had been already prepared by correspondence and petition. His *Hope of Israel* had been forwarded to Cromwell so

early as 1650; petitions praying for the readmission of Jews to England with full rights
of worship, of burial, and of commerce secured
to them, had been laid before the Long and
the Rump Parliament, and Manasseh had now
in hand, and approaching completion, a less
elaborate and more impassioned composition
than usual, entitled, *Vindiciæ Judæorum*. A
powerful and unexpected advocate of Jewish
claims presently came forward in the person
of Edward Nicholas, the clerk to the Council.
This large-minded and enlightened gentleman
had the courage to publish an elaborate appeal
for, and defence of, the Jews, 'the most
honourable people in the world,' as he styled
them, 'a people chosen by God and protected
by God.' The pamphlet was headed, *Apology for the Honourable Nation of the Jews
and all the Sons of Israel*, and Nicholas's
arguments aroused no small amount of attention and discussion. It was even whispered
that Cromwell had had a share in the author-
ship; but if this had been so, undoubtedly he
who 'stood bare, not cased in euphemistic
coat of mail,' but who 'grappled like a giant,
face to face, heart to heart, with the naked
truth of things,'[1] would have unhesitatingly
avowed it. His was not the sort of nature to
shirk responsibilities nor to lack the courage

[1] *On Heroes*: Lect. vi., 'The Hero as King,' . 342.

of his opinions. There can be no doubt that, from first to last, Cromwell was strongly in favour of Jewish claims being allowed, but just as little doubt is there that there was never any tinge or taint of ' secret favouring ' about his sayings or his doings on the subject. The part, and all things considered the very unpopular part, he took in the subsequent debates, had, of course, to be accounted for by minds not quick to understand such simple motive power as justice, generosity, or sympathy, and both now and later the wildest accusations were levelled against the Protector. That he was, unsuspected, himself of Jewish descent, and had designs on the long vacant Messiahship of his interesting kinsfolk, was not the most malignant, though it was perhaps among the most absurd, of these tales. 'The man is without a soul,' writes Carlyle, 'that can look into the great soul of a man, radiant with the splendours of very heaven, and see nothing there but the shadow of his own mean darkness.'[1] There must have been, if this view be correct, a good many particularly materialistic bodies going about at that epoch in English history when the Protector of England took upon himself the unpopular burden of being also the Protector of the Jews.

[1] *Cromwell*, vol. ii. p. 359.

F

There had been some opposition on the part of the family to overcome, some tender timid forebodings, which events subsequently justified, to dispel, before Manasseh was free to set out for England; but in the late autumn of 1655[1] we find him with two or three companions safely settled in lodgings in the Strand. An address to the Protector was personally presented by Manasseh, whilst a more detailed declaration to the Commonwealth was simultaneously published. Very remarkable are both these documents. Neither in the personal petition to Cromwell, nor in the more elaborate argument addressed to the Parliament, is there the slightest approach to the *ad misericordiam* style. The whole case for the Jews is stated with dignity, and pleaded without passion, and throughout justice rather than favour forms the staple of the demand. The 'clemency' and 'high-mindedness' of Cromwell are certainly taken for granted, but equally is assumed the worthiness of the clients who appeal to these qualities. Manasseh makes also a strong point of the 'Profit,' which the Jews are likely to prove to their hosts, naïvely recognising the fact that 'Profit is a most powerful motive which all the world prefers above all other things'; and 'therefore dealing with that

----

[1] Some chroniclers fix it so early as 1653.

point first.' He dwells on the 'ability,' and 'industry,' and 'natural instinct' of the Jews for 'merchandising,' and for 'contributing new inventions,' which extra aptitude, in a somewhat optimistic spirit, he moralises, may have been given to them for their 'protection in their wanderings,' since 'wheresoever they go to dwell, there presently the traficq begins to flourish.'

Read in the light of some recent literature, one or two of Manasseh's arguments might almost be termed prophetic. Far-sighted, however, and wide-seeing as was our Amsterdam Rabbi, he could certainly not have foretold that more than two hundred years later his race would be taunted in the same breath for being a 'wandering' and 'homeless tribe,' and for remaining a 'settled' and 'parasitic' people in their adopted countries; yet are not such ingenious, and ungenerous, and inconsistent taunts answered by anticipation in the following paragraph?—

'The love that men ordinarily bear to their own country, and the desire they have to end their lives where they had their beginning, is the cause that most strangers, having gotten riches where they are in a foreign land, are commonly taken in a desire to return to their native soil, and there peaceably to enjoy their

estate ; so that as they were a help to the
places where they lived and negotiated while
they remained there, so when they depart
from thence, they carry all away and spoile
them of their wealth ; transporting all into
their own native country : but with the Jews,
the case is farre different, for where the Jews
are once kindly receaved, they make a firm
resolution never to depart from thence, seeing
they have no proper place of their own ; and
so they are always with their goods in the
cities where they live, a perpetual benefitt to
all payments.' [1]

Manasseh goes on to quote Holy Writ, to
show that to 'seek for the peace,' and to 'pray
for the peace of the city whither ye are led
captive,' [2] was from remote times a loyal duty
enjoined on Jews; and so he makes perhaps
another point against that thorough-going
historian of our day, who would have disposed
of the People and the Book, the Jews and the
Old Testament together, in the course of a
magazine article.   To prove that uncompromising loyalty has among the Jews the added
force of a religious obligation, Manasseh
mentions the fact that the ruling dynasty is
always prayed for by upstanding congregations

---

[1] From 'Declaration to the Commonwealth of England.'
[2] Jeremiah xxix. 7.

in every Jewish place of worship, and he makes
history give its evidence to show that this is
no mere lip loyalty, but that the obligation
enjoined has been over and over again faithfully fulfilled.   He quotes numerous instances
in proof of this; beginning from the time, 900
years B.C., when the Jerusalem Jews, High
Priest at their head, went forth to defy Alex-
ander, and to own staunch allegiance to
discrowned Darius, till those recent civil wars
in Spain, when the Jews of Burgos manfully
held that city against the conqueror, Henry of
Trastamare, in defence of their conquered,
but liege lord, Pedro.[1]

Of all the simply silly slanders from which
his people had suffered, such, for instance, as
the kneading Passover biscuits with the blood
of Christian children, Manasseh disposes
shortly, with brief and distinct denial; per-
tinently reminding Englishmen, however, that
like absurd accusations crop up in the early
history of the Church, when the 'very same
ancient scandalls was cast of old upon the
innocent Christians.'

With the more serious, because less absolutely untruthful, charge of 'usury,' Manasseh
deals as boldly, urging even no extenuating
plea, but frankly admitting the practice to be
'infamous.'   But characteristically, he pro-

---

[1] In 1369.

ceeds to express an opinion, that 'inasmuch as no man is bound to give his goods to another, so is he not bound to let it out but for his own occasions and profit,' 'only,' and this he adds emphatically—

'It must be done with moderation, that the usury be not biting or exorbitant. . . . The sacred Scripture, which allows usury with him that is not of the same religion, forbids absolutely the robbing of all men, whatso-ever religion they be of. In our law it is a greater sinne to rob or defraud a stranger, than if I did it to one of my owne profession ; a Jew is bound to show his charity to all men ; he hath a precept, not to abhorre an Idumean or an Egyptian ; and yet another, that he shall love and protect a stranger that comes to live in his land. If, notwithstanding, there be some that do contrary to this, they do it not as Jewes simply, but as wicked Jewes.'

The Appeal made, as it could scarcely fail to do, a profound impression—an impression which was helped not a little by the presence and character of the pleader. And presently the whole question of the return of the Jews to England was submitted to the nation for its decision.

The clergy were dead against the measure,

and, it is said, 'raged like fanatics against the Jews as an accursed nation.' And then it was that Cromwell, true to his highest convictions, stood up to speak in their defence. On the ground of policy, he temperately urged the desirability of adding thrifty, law-respecting, and enterprising citizens to the national stock; and on the higher ground of duty, he passionately pleaded the unpopular cause of religious and social toleration. He deprecated the principle that, the claims of morality being satisfied, any men or any body of men, on the score of race, of origin, or of religion ('tribal mark' had not at that date been suggested), should be excluded from full fellowship with other men. 'I have never heard a man speak so splendidly in my life,' is the recorded opinion of one of the audience, and it is a matter of intense regret that this famous speech of Cromwell's has not been preserved. Its eloquence, however, failed of effect, so far as its whole and immediate object was concerned. The gates were no more than shaken on their rusting hinges—not quite yet were the people free to 'go through.'

The decision of the Council of State was deferred, and some authorities even allege that it was presently pronounced against the readmission of the Jews to England. The known and avowed favour of the Protector sufficed, nevertheless, to induce the few Jews who had come with, or in the train of, Manasseh to remain, and others gradually, and by degrees, and without any especial notice being taken of them, ventured to follow. The creaking old gates were certainly ajar, and wider and wider they opened, and fainter and fainter, from friction of unrestrained intercourse, grew each dull rust and stain of prejudice, till that good day, within living memories, when the barriers were definitely and altogether flung down. And on their ruins a new and healthy human growth sprang quickly up, 'taking root downwards, and fruit upwards,' spreading wide enough in its vigorous luxuriance to cover up all the old bad past. And by this time it has happily grown impervious to any wanton unfriendly touch which would thrust its kindly shade aside and once again lay those ugly ruins bare.

Manasseh, however, like so many of us, had to be content to sow seed which he was destined never to see ripen. His petitions to the Commonwealth were presented in 1655, his *Vindiciæ Judæorum* was completed and handed in some time in 1656, and in the early winter of 1657, on his journey homewards, he died. His mission had not fulfilled itself in the complete triumphant way he had hoped, but 'life fulfils itself in many ways,' and one part at

any rate, perhaps the most important part, of
the Hebrew prophet's charge, had been both
poetically and prosaically carried out by this
seventeenth century Dutch Jew.   He had
'lifted up a standard for his people.'

CHARITY IN TALMUDIC TIMES

SOME ANCIENT SOLVINGS OF A MODERN PROBLEM

'WHAT have we reaped from all the wisdom sown of ages?' asks Lord Lytton in one of his earlier poems. A large query, even for so questioning an age as this, an age which, discarding catechisms, and rejecting the omniscient Mangnall's Questions as a classic for its children, yet seems to be more interrogative than of old, even if a thought less ready in its responses. Possibly, we are all in too great a hurry nowadays, too eager in search to be patient to find, for certain it is that the world's already large stock of hows and whys seems to get bigger every day. We catch the echoes in poetry and in prose, in all sorts of tones and from all sorts of people, and Lord Lytton's question sounds only like another of the hopeless Pilate series. His is such a large interrogation too—all the wisdom sown of all the ages suggests such an enormous crop! And then as to what 'we,' who have neither planted nor watered, have 'reaped' from it! An answer, if it were attempted, might certainly be found to hinge on the 'we' as well as on the 'wisdom,' for whereas untaught instinct may 'reap' honey from a rose, trained reason in gathering the flower may only succeed in running a thorn into the finger. What has been the general effect of inherited wisdom on the general world may, however, very well be left for a possible solution to prize competitors to puzzle over. But to a tiny corner of the tremendous subject it is just possible that we may find some sort of suggestive reply; and from seed sown ages since, and garnered as harvest by men whose place knows them no more, we may likely light on some shadowy aftermath worth, perhaps, our reaping.

The gospel of duty to one's neighbour, which, long languishing as a creed, seems now reviving as a fashion, has always been, amongst that race which taught 'love thy neighbour as thyself,' not only of the very essence of religion, but an ordinary social form of it. It is 'law' in the 'family chronicle' of the race, as Heine calls the Bible; it is 'law' and legend both in those curious national archives known as Talmud. Foremost in the ranks of *livres incompris* stand those portentous volumes, the one work of the world which has suffered about equally at the hands of the commen-

tator and the executioner. Many years ago
Emmanuel Deutsch gave to the uninitiated a
glimpse into that wondrous agglomeration of
fantastically followed facts, where long-winded
legend, or close-argued 'law,' starts some
phrase or word from Holy Writ as quarry, and
pursues it by paths the most devious, the
most digressive imaginable to man. The work
of many generations and of many 'masters' in
each generation, such a book is singularly
susceptible to an open style of reading and
a liberal aptitude of quotation, and it is
no marvel that searchers in its pages, even
reasonably honest ones, should be able to
find detached individual utterances to fit into
almost any one of their own preconceived
dogmas concerning Talmud. On many subjects, qualifications, contradictions, differences
abound, and instances of illegal law, of pseudo-
science, of doubtful physics, may each, with a
little trouble, be disinterred from the depths
of these twelve huge volumes. But the ethics
of the Talmud are, as a whole, of a high order,
and on one point there is such remarkable and
entire agreement, that it is here permissible
to speak of what 'the Talmud says,' meaning
thereby a general tone and consensus of
opinion, and not the views of this or of that
individual master. The subject on which this
unusual harmony prevails is the, in these days,

much discussed one of charity; and to discover something concerning so very ancient a mode of dealing with it may not prove uninteresting.

The word which in these venerable folios is made to express the thing is, in itself, significant. In the Hebrew Scriptures, though the injunctions to charitable acts are many, an exact equivalent to our word 'charity' can hardly be said to exist. In only eight instances, and not even then in its modern sense, does the Septuagint translate צדקה (*tzedakah*) into its Greek equivalent, ἐλεημοσύνη, which would become in English 'alms,' or 'charity.' The nearest synonyms for 'charity' in the Hebrew Scriptures are צרקה (*tzedakah*), well translated as 'righteousness' in the Authorised Version, and חסר (*chesed*), which is adequately rendered as 'mercy, kindness, love.' The Talmud, in its exhaustive fashion, seems to accentuate the essential difference between these two words. *Tzedakah* is, to some extent, a class distinction; the rights of the poor make occasion for the righteousness of the rich, and the duties of *tzedakah* find liberal and elaborate expression in a strict and minute system of tithes and almsgiving.[1] The injunctions of the Penta-

---

[1] Maimonides, in his well-known digest of Talmudic laws relating to the poor, uniformly employs *tzedakah* in the sense of 'alms.'

teuch concerning the poor are worked out by
the Talmud into the fullest detail of direction.
The Levitical law, 'When ye reap the harvest
of your land, thou shalt not wholly reap the
corners of thy field' (Levit. xiv. 9), gives
occasion of itself to a considerable quantity of
literature. At length, it is enacted how, if
brothers divide a field between them, each has
to give a 'corner,' and how, if a man sell his
field in several lots, each purchaser of each
separate lot has to leave unreaped his own
proportionate 'corner' of the harvesting. And
not only to leave unreaped, but how, in cases
where the 'corner' was of a sort hard for the
poor to gather, hanging high, as dates, or
needing light handling, as grapes, it became
the duty of the owner to undertake the 'reaping' thereof, and, himself, to make the rightful
division; thus guarding against injury to
quickly perishable fruits from too eager hands,
or danger of a more serious sort to life or limbs,
where ladders had to be used by hungry and
impatient folks. The exactest rules, too, are
formulated as to what constitutes a 'field' and
what a 'corner,' as to what produce is liable to
the tax and in what measure. Very curious it
is to read long and gravely reasoned arguments
as to why mushrooms should be held exempt
from the law of the corner, whilst onions must
be subject to it, or the weighty *pros* and

cons over what may be fairly considered a
'fallen grape,' or a 'sheaf left through forget-
fulness.' Yet the principle underlying the
whole is too clear for prolixity to raise a smile,
and the evident anxiety that no smallest loop-
hole shall be left for evading the obligations
of property compels respect.

Little room for doubt on any disputed point
of partition do these exhaustive, and, occasionally, it must be owned, exhausting, masters
leave us, yet, when all is said, they are careful
to add, 'Whatever is doubtful concerning the
gifts of the poor belongeth to the poor.' The
actual money value of this system of alms, the
actual weight of ancient ephah or omer, in
modern lbs. and ozs. would convey little meaning. Values fluctuate and measures vary, but 'a
tithe of thy increase,' 'a corner of thy field,'
gives a tolerably safe index to the scale on
which *tzedakah* was to be practised. Three
times a day the poor might glean, and to the
question which some lover of system, old style
or new, might propound, 'Why three times?
Why not once, and get it over?' an answer is
vouchsafed. *Because there may be poor who are
suckling children, and thus stand in need of food
in the early morning; there may be young children
who cannot be got ready early in the morning, nor
come to the field till it be mid-day; there may be
aged folk who cannot come till the time of evening*

prayer.' Still, though plenty of sentiment in
this code, there is no trace of sentimentality;
rather a tendency for each back to bear its
own burden, whether it be in the matter of
give or take. Rights are respected all round,
and significant in this sense is the rule that if
a vineyard be sold by Gentile to Jew it must
give up its 'small bunches' of grapes to the
poor; while if the transaction be the other
way, the Gentile purchaser is altogether
exempt, and if Jew and Gentile be partners,
that part of the crop belonging to the Jew
alone is taxed. And equally clear is it that
the poor, though cared for and protected, are
not to be petted. At this very three-times-a-
day gleaning, if one should keep a corner of
his 'corner' to himself, hiding his harvesting
and defrauding his neighbour, justice is
prompt: *'Let him be forced to depart,'* it is
written, *'and what he may have received let it be
taken out of his hands.'* Neither is any preference
permitted to poverty of the plausible or of the
picturesque sort: *'He who refuseth to one and
giveth to another, that man is a defrauder of the
poor,'* it is gravely said.

In general charity, there are, it is true,
certain rules of precedence to be observed;
kindred, for example, have, in all cases, the
first claim, and a child supporting his parents,
or even a parent supporting adult children, to

the end that these may be 'versed in the law, and have good manners,' is set high among followers of *tzedakah*. Then, ' *The poor who are neighbours are to be regarded before all others ; the poor of one's own family before the poor of one's own city, and the poor of one's own city before the poor of another's city.'* And this version of ' charity begins at home' is worked out in another place into quite a detailed table, so to speak, of professional precedence in the ranks of recognised recipients. And, curiously enough, first among all the distinctions to be observed comes this: '*If a man and woman solicit relief, the woman shall be first attended to and then the man.'* An explanation, perhaps a justi-fication, of this mild forestalment of women's rights, is given in the further dictum that ' Man is accustomed to wander, and that woman is not,' and ' Her feelings of modesty being more acute,' it is fit that she should be ' always fed and clothed before the man.' And if, in this ancient system, there be a recognised scale of rights for receiving, so, equally, is there a graduated order of merit in giving. Eight in number are these so-called ' Degrees in Alms Deeds,' the curious list gravely setting forth as ' highest,' and this, it would seem, rather on the lines of 'considering the poor' than of mere giving, that *tzedakah* which ' helpeth . . . who is cast down,' by means of gift or loan, or timely procuring of employment, and ranging through 'next' and 'next,' till it announces, as eighth and least, the 'any one who giveth after much molestation.' High in the list, too, are placed those 'silent givers' who 'let not poor children of upright parents know from whom they receive support,' and even the man who 'giveth less than his means allow' is lifted one degree above the lowest if he 'give with a kind countenance.'

The mode of relief grew, with circumstances, to change. The time came when, to 'the Hagars and Ishmaels of mankind,' rules for gleaning and for 'fallen grapes' would, perforce, be meaningless, and new means for the carrying out of *tzedakah* had to be devised. In Alms of the Chest, קופה (*kupah*), and Alms of the Basket, תמחוי (*tamchui*), another exhaustive system of relief was formulated. The *kupah* would seem to have been a poor-rate, levied on all 'residents in towns of over thirty days' standing,' and 'Never,' says Maimonides, 'have we seen or heard of any congregation of Israelites in which there has not been the Chest for Alms, though, with regard to the Basket, it is the custom in some places to have it, and not in others.' These chests were placed in the Silent Court of the Sanctuary, to the end that a class of givers who went

by the name of Fearers of Sin,[1] might deposit
their alms in silence and be relieved of re-
sponsibility.   The contents of the Chest were
collected weekly and used for all ordinary
objects of relief, the overplus being devoted to
special cases and special purposes.   It is somewhat strange to our modern notions to find
that one among such purposes was that of
providing poor folks with the wherewith to
marry.   For not only is it commanded concerning the 'brother waxen poor,' ' *If he standeth in
need of garments, let him be clothed ; or if of
household things, let him be supplied with them,*'
but '*if of a wife, let a wife be betrothed unto him,
and in case of a woman, let a husband be betrothed
unto her.*'   Does this quaint provision recall
Voltaire's taunt that 'Les juifs ont toujours
regardé comme leurs deux grands devoirs des
enfants et de l'argent'?   Perhaps, and yet,
Voltaire and even Malthus notwithstanding, it
is just possible that the last word has not been
said on this subject, and that in ' improvident '
marriages and large families the new creed of
survival of the fittest may, after all, be best
fulfilled.

Philosophers, we know, are not always con-

---

[1] יראי חטא (*yerce chet*).   These ultra-sensitive folks
seem to have feared that in direct relief they might be
imposed on and so indirectly become encouragers of wrong-
doing, or unnecessarily hurt the feelings of the poor by too
rigid inquiries.

sistent with themselves, and if there be truth in another saying of Voltaire's—'Voyez les registres affreux de vos greffes crimines, vous y trouvez cent garçons de pendus ou de roués contre un père de famille '—then is there something certainly to be said in favour of the Jewish system. But this by the way, since statistics, it must be owned, are the most sensitive and susceptible of the sciences. This ancient betrothing, moreover, was no empty form, no bare affiancing of two paupers ; but a serious and substantial practice of raising a marriage portion for a couple unable to marry without it. By Talmudic code, 'marriages were not legitimately complete till a settlement of some sort was made on the wife,' who, it may be here parenthetically remarked, was so far in advance of comparatively modern legislation as to be entitled to have and to hold in as complete and comprehensive a sense as her husband.

But whilst Alms of the Chest, though pretty various in its application,[1] was intended only

[1] We read, in mediæval times, of the existence of wide 'extensions' of this system of relief. In a curious old book, published in the seventeenth century, by a certain Rabbi Elijah ha Cohen ben Abraham, of Smyrna, we find a list drawn up of Jewish charities to which, as he says, 'all pious Jews contribute.' These modes of satisfying 'the hungry soul' are over seventy in number, and of the most various kinds. They include the lending of money

for the poor of the place in which it was collected, Alms of the Basket was, to the extent
of its capabilities, for 'the poor of the whole
world.' It consisted of a daily house-to-house
collection of food of all sorts, and occasionally
of money, which was again, day by day, distributed. This custom of *tamchui*, suited to those
primitive times, would seem to be very similar
to the practice of ' common Boxes, and common
gatherynges in every City,' which prevailed in
England in the sixteenth century, and which
received legal sanction in Act of the 23rd of
Henry VIII.—' Item, that 2 or 3 tymes in
every weke 2 or 3 of every parysh shal appoynt
certaine of ye said pore people to collecte and
gather broken meates and fragments, and the
refuse drynke of every householder, which
shal be distributed evenly amonge the pore
people as they by theyre discrecyons shal
thynke good.' Only the collectors and distri-
butors of *kupah* and *tamchui* were not ' certaine
of ye said pore people,' but unpaid men of
high character, holding something of the
position of magistrates in the community.
The duty of contributing in kind to *tamchui*
was supplemented among the richer folks

and the lending of books, the payment of dowries and the
payment of burial charges, doctors' fees for the sick,
legal fees for the unjustly accused, ransom for captives,
ornaments for bribes, and wet nurses for orphans.

by a habit of entertaining the poor as
guests;[1] seats at their own tables, and
beds in their houses being frequently reserved for wayfarers, at least over Sabbath
and festivals.[2]

The curious union of sense and sentiment
in the Talmudic code is shown again in the
regulations as to who may, and who may not,
receive of these gifts of the poor: '*He who has
sufficient for two meals,*' so runs the law, '*may
not take from tamchui; he who has sufficient for
fourteen may not take from kupah.*' Yet might
holders of property, fallen on slack seasons, be
saved from selling at a loss and helped to hold
on till better times, by being ' meanwhile sup-
ported out of the tithes of the poor.' And if
the house and goods of him in this temporary
need were grand, money help might be given
to the applicant, and he might keep all his
smart personal belongings, yet superfluities, an
odd item or two of which are vouchsafed, must
be sold, and replaced, if at all, by a simpler
sort. Still, with all this excessive care for

---

[1] Spanish Jews often had their coffins made from the
wood of the tables at which they had sat with their unfashionable guests.

[2] This custom had survived into quite modern times—to
cite only the well-known case of Mendelssohn, who, coming as a penniless student to Berlin, received his Sabbath
meals in the house of one co-religionist, and the privilege
of an attic chamber under the roof of another.

those who have come down in the world, and despite the dictum that 'he who withholdeth alms is "impious" and like unto an idolater,' there is yet no encouragement to dependence discernible in these precise and prolix rules. 'Let thy Sabbath be as an ordinary day, rather than become dependent on thy fellow-men,' it is clearly written, and told, too, in detail, how 'wise men,' the most honoured, by the way, in the community, to avoid 'dependence on others,' might become, without loss of caste or respectability, 'carriers of timber, workers in metal, and makers of charcoal.' Neither is there any contempt for wealth or any love of poverty for its own sake to be seen in this people, who were taught to 'rejoice before the Lord.' In one place it is, in truth, gravely set forth that 'he who increaseth the number of his servants' increaseth the amount of sin in the world, but this somewhat ascetic-sounding statement is clearly susceptible of a good deal of common-sense interpretation, and when another Master tells us that 'charity is the salt which keeps wealth from corruption,' a thought, perhaps, for the due preservation of the wealth may be read between the lines.

On the whole, it looks as if these old-world Rabbis set to work at laying down the law in much the spirit of Robert Browning's Rabbi—

'Let us not always say,
　　Spite of this flesh to-day,
I strove, made head, gained ground upon the whole.
　　As the bird wings and sings
　　Let us cry, 'All good things
Are ours, nor soul helps flesh more now than flesh
　　helps soul.'

After this manner, at any rate, are set forth, and in this sense are interpreted in the Talmud, the Biblical injunctions to *tzedakah*, to that charity of alms-deeds which, as society is constituted, must, as we said, be considered somewhat of a class distinction.

But for the charity which should be obligatory all round, and as easy of fulfilment by the poor as by the rich, the Talmud chooses the other synonym חסד (*chesed*), and coining from it the word *Gemiluth-chesed*, which may be rendered 'the doing of kindness,' it works out a supplementary and social system of charity—a system founded not on 'rights,' but on sympathy—dealing not in doles, but in deeds of friendship and of fellowship, and demanding a giving of oneself rather than of one's stores. And greater than *tzedakah*, write the Rabbis, is *Gemiluth-chesed*, justifying their dictum, as is their wont, by a reference to Holy Writ. 'Sow to yourselves in righteousness (*tzedakah*),' says the prophet Hosea (Hos. x. 12); 'reap in mercy (*chesed*)'; and, inasmuch as reaping is better than sowing, mercy must be better than righteousness. To 'visit the sick,' to promote peace in families apt to fall out, to 'relieve all persons, Jews or non-Jews, in affliction' (a comprehensive phrase), to 'bury the dead,' to 'accompany the bride,' are among those 'kindnesses' which take rank as religious duties, and one or two specimens may indicate the amount of careful detail which make these injunctions practical, and the fine motive which goes far towards spiritualising them.

Of the visiting of the sick, the Talmud speaks with a sort of awe. God's spirit, it says, dwells in the chamber of suffering and death, and tendance therein is worship. Nursing was to be voluntary, and no charge to be made for drugs; and so deeply did the habit of helping the helpless in this true missionary spirit obtain among the Jews, that to this day, and more especially in provincial places, the last offices for the dead are rarely performed by hired hands. The 'accompanying of the bride' is *Gemiluth-chesed* in another form. To rejoice with one's neighbour's joys is no less a duty in this un-Rochefoucauld-like code than to grieve with his grief. A bride is to be greeted with songs and flowers, and pleasant speeches, and, if poor, to be provided with pretty ornaments and substantial gifts, but the pleasant speeches are in all cases, and before all things, obligatory. In the discursive detail, which is so strong a feature of these Talmudic rulings, it is asked: 'But if the bride be old, or awkward, or positively plain, is she to be greeted in the usual formula as "fair bride—graceful bride"?' 'Yes,' is the answer, for one is not bound to insist on uncomfortable facts, nor to be obtrusively truthful; to be agreeable is one of the minor virtues. Were there anything in the doctrine of metempsychosis, one would be almost tempted to believe that this ancient unnamed Rabbi was speaking over again in the person of one of our modern minor poets:

> 'A truth that's told with bad intent
> Beats all the lies you can invent.'[1]

The charity of courtesy is everywhere insisted upon, and so strongly, that, on behalf of those sometimes ragged and unkempt Rabbis it might perhaps be urged that politeness, the *politesse du cœur*, was their Judaism *en papillote*. 'Receive every one with pleasant looks,' says one sage,[2] whose practice was, perhaps, not always quite up to his precepts; 'where there is no reverence there is no wisdom,' says another; and as the distinguishing mark of a 'clown,' a third instances that

---

[1] William Blake.   [2] Shimei.

man—have we not all met him?—who rudely breaks in on another's speech, and is more glib than accurate or respectful in his own.

And as postscript to the 'law' obtaining on these cheery social forms of 'charity' a tombstone may perhaps be permitted to add its curious crumbling bit of evidence. In the House of Life, as Jews name their burialgrounds, at Prague, there stood—perhaps stands still—a stone, erected to the memory, and recording the virtues, of a certain rich lady who died in 1628. Her benefactions, many and minute, are set forth at length, and amongst the rest, and before 'she clothed the naked,' comes the item, 'she ran like a bird to weddings.' Through the mists of those terrible stories, which make of Prague so miserable a memory to Jews, the record of this long-ago dead woman gleams like a rainbow. One seems to see the bright little figure, a trifle out of breath may be, the gay plumage perhaps just a shade ruffled—somehow one does not fancy her a very prim or tidy personage—running 'like a bird to weddings.' She seems, the dear sympathetic soul, in an odd, suggestive sort of way, to illustrate the charitable system of her race, and to show us that, despite all differences of time and place and circumstances, the one essential condition to any 'charity' that shall prove effectual remains unchanged; that the solution of the hard problem, which may be worked out in a hundred ways, is just sympathy, and is to be learnt, not in the 'speaking from afar' of rich to poor, but in the 'laying of hands' upon them. The close fellowship of this ancient primitive system is perhaps impossible in our more complex civilisation, but an approximation to it is an ideal worth striving after. More intimate, more everyday communion between West and East, more 'Valentines' at Hoxton are sorely needed. Concert-giving, class-teaching, 'visiting,' are all helps of a sort, but there are so many days in a poor man's week, so many hours in his dull day. Sweetness and light, like other and more prosaic products of civilisation, need, it may be, to be 'laid on' in those miles of monotonous streets, long breaks in continuity being fatal to results.

'I wish, it is true, to shame the opprobrious
sentiments commonly entertained of a Jew,
but it is by character and not by controversy
that I would do it.'[1] So wrote the subject of
this memoir more than a hundred years ago,
and the sentence may well stand for the motto
of his life; for much as Moses Mendelssohn
achieved by his ability, much more did he by
his conduct, and great as he was as a philosopher, far greater was he as a man.   Starting
with every possible disadvantage—prejudice,
poverty, and deformity—he yet reached the
goal of 'honour, fame, and troops of friends'
by simple force of character; and thus he
remains for all time an illustration of the
happy optimistic theory that, even in this
world, success, in the best sense of the word,
does come to those who, also in the best
sense of the word, deserve it.

The state of the Jews in Germany at the
time of Mendelssohn's birth was deplorable.
No longer actively hunted, they had arrived,
at the early part of the eighteenth century, at

[1] In the correspondence with Lavater.

the comparatively desirable position of being passively shunned or contemptuously ignored, and, under these new conditions, they were narrowing fast to the narrow limits set them. The love of religion and of race was as strong as ever, but the love had grown sullen, and of that jealous, exclusive sort to which curse and anathema are akin. What then loomed largest on their narrow horizon was fear; and under that paralysing influence, progress or prominence of any kind became a distinct evil, to be repressed at almost any personal sacrifice. Safety for themselves and tolerance for their faith, lay, if anywhere, in the neglect of the outside world. And so the poor pariahs huddled in their close quarters, carrying on mean trades, or hawking petty wares, and speaking, with bated breath, a dialect of their own, half Jewish, half German, and as wholly degenerate from the grand old Hebrew as were they themselves from those to whom it had been a living tongue. Intellectual occupation was found in the study of the Law; interest and entertainment in the endless discussion of its more intricate passages; and excitement in the not infrequent excommunication of the weaker or bolder brethren who ventured to differ from the orthodox expounders. The culture of the Christian they hated, with a hate born half of

fear for its possible effects, half of repulsion at
its palpable evidences. The tree of knowledge
seemed to them indeed, in pathetic perversion
of the early legend, a veritable tree of evil,
which should lose a second Eden to the wilful
eaters thereof.   Their Eden was degenerate
too ; but the ' voice heard in the evening ' still
sounded in their dulled and passionate ears,
and, vibrating in the Ghetto instead of the
grove, it seemed to bid them shun the for-
bidden fruit of Gentile growth.

In September 1729, under a very humble
roof, in a very poor little street in Dessau, was
born the weakly boy who was destined to work
such wonderful changes in that weary state of
things.   Not much fit to hold the magician's
wand seemed those frail baby hands, and less
and less likely altogether for the part, as the
poor little body grew stunted and deformed
through the stress of over-much study and of
something less than enough of wholesome
diet.   There was no lack of affection in the
mean little Jewish home, but the parents could
only give their children of what they had, and
of these scant possessions, mother-love and Tal-
mudical lore were the staple.   And so we read
of the small five-year-old Moses being wrapped
up by his mother in a large old shabby cloak,
on early, bleak winter mornings, and then so
carried by the father to the neighbouring

'Talmud Torah' school, where he was nourished
with dry Hebrew roots by way of breakfast.
Often, indeed, was the child fed on an even
less satisfying diet, for long passages from
Scripture, long lists of precepts, to be learnt
by heart, on all sorts of subjects, was the
approved method of instruction in these
seminaries. An extensive, if somewhat parrot-
like, acquaintance at an astonishingly early
age with the Law and the Prophets, and the
commentators on both, was the ordinary result
of this form of education; and, naturally co-
existent with it, was an equally astonishing
and extensive ignorance of all more everyday
subjects. Contentedly enough, however, the
learned, illiterate peddling and hawking fathers
left their little lads to this puzzling, sharpening,
deadening sort of schooling. Frau Mendel and
her husband may possibly have thought out
the matter a little more fully, for she seems
to have been a wise and prudent as well as a
loving mother; and the father, we find, was
quick to discern unusual talent in the sickly
little son whom he carried so carefully to the
daily lesson. He was himself a teacher, in a
humble sort of way, and eked out his small
fees by transcribing on parchment from the
Pentateuch. Thus, the tone of the little
household, if not refined, was at least not
altogether sordid; and when, presently, the

little Moses was promoted from the ordinary
school to the higher class taught by the great
scholar, Rabbi Frankel, the question even
presented itself whether it might not be well,
in this especial case, to abandon the patent,
practical advantages pertaining to the favoured
pursuit of peddling, and to let the boy give
himself up to his beloved books, and, following
in his master's footsteps, become perhaps, in his
turn, a poorly paid, much reverenced Rabbi.

It was a serious matter to decide. There
was much to be said in favour of the higher
path; but the market for Rabbis, as for
hawkers, was somewhat overstocked, and the
returns in the one instance were far quicker
and surer, and needed no long unearning
apprenticeship. The balance, on the whole,
seemed scarcely to incline to the more dignified
profession; but the boy was so terribly in
earnest in his desire to learn, so desperately
averse from the only other career, that his
wishes, by degrees, turned the scale; and it
did not take very long to convince the poor
patient father that he must toil a little longer
and a little later, in order that his son might
be free from the hated necessity of hawking,
and at liberty to pursue his unremunerative
studies.

From the very first, Moses made the most
of his opportunities; and at home and at

school high hopes began soon to be formed of
the diligent, sweet-tempered, frail little lad.
Frailer than ever, though, he seemed to grow,
and the body appeared literally to dwindle as
the mind expanded. Long years after, when
the burden of increasing deformity had come,
by dint of use and wont and cheerful courage,
to be to him a burden lightly borne, he would
set strangers at their ease by alluding to it
himself, and by playfully declaring his hump
to be a legacy from Maimonides. 'Maimonides spoilt my figure,' he would say, 'and
ruined my digestion; but still,' he would add
more seriously, 'I dote on him, for although
those long vigils with him weakened my body,
they, at the same time, strengthened my soul:
they stunted my stature, but they developed
my mind.' Early at morning and late at
night would the boy be found bending in
happy abstraction over his shabby treasure,
charmed into unconsciousness of aches or
hunger. The book, which had been lent to
him, was Maimonides' *Guide to the Perplexed*;
and this work, which grown men find sufficiently
deep study, was patiently puzzled out, and
enthusiastically read and re-read by the per-
severing little student who was barely in his
teens. It opened up whole vistas of new
glories, which his long steady climb up Talmudic stairs had prepared him to appreciate.

Here and there, in the course of those long, tedious dissertations in the Talmud Torah class-room, the boy had caught glimpses of something underlying, something beyond the quibbles of the schools; but this, his first insight into the large and liberal mind of Maimonides, was a revelation to him of the powers and of the possibilities of Judaism. It revealed to him too, perchance, some latent possibilities in himself, and suggested other problems of life which asked solution. The pale cheeks glowed as he read, and the vague dreams kindled into conscious aims: he too would live to become a Guide to the Perplexed among his people!

Poor little lad! his brave resolves were soon to be put to a severe test. In the early part of 1742, Rabbi Frankel accepted the Chief Rabbinate of Berlin, and thus a summary stop was put to his pupil's further study. There is a pathetic story told of Moses Mendelssohn standing, with streaming eyes, on a little hillock on the road by which his beloved master passed out of Dessau, and of the kind-hearted Frankel catching up the forlorn little figure, and soothing it with hopes of a 'some day,' when fortune should be kind, and he should follow 'nach Berlin.' The 'some day' looked sadly problematical; that hard question of bread and butter came to the fore whenever it was discussed. How was the boy to live in Berlin? Even if the mind should be nourished for naught, who was to feed the body? The hard-working father and mother had found it no easy task hitherto to provide for that extra mouth; and now, with Frankel gone, the occasion for their long self-denial seemed to them to cease. In the sad straits of the family, the business of a hawker began again to show in an attractive light to the poor parents, and the pedlar's pack was once more suggested with many a prudent, loving, half-hearted argument on its behalf. But the boy was by this time clear as to his vocation, so after a brief while of entreaty, the tearful permission was gained, the parting blessing given, and with a very slender wallet slung on his crooked shoulders, Moses Mendelssohn set out for Berlin.

It was a long tramp of over thirty miles, and, towards the close of the fifth day, it was a very footsore, tired little lad who presented himself for admission at the Jews' gate of the city. Rabbi Frankel was touched, and puzzled too, when this penniless little student, whom he had inspired with such difficult devotion, at last stood before him; but quickly he made up his mind that, so far as in him lay, the uphill path should be made smooth to those determined little feet. The pressing question of bed and board was solved. Frankel gave him his Sabbath and festival dinners, and another kind-hearted Jew, Bamberger by name, who heard the boy's story, supplied two everyday meals, and let him sleep in an attic in his house. For the remaining four days? Well, he managed; a groschen or two was often earned by little jobs of copying, and a loaf so purchased, by dint of economy and imagination, was made into quite a series of satisfying meals, and, in after-days, it was told how he notched his loaves into accurate time measurements, lest appetite should outrun purse. Fortunately poverty was no new experience for him; still, poverty confronted alone, in a great city, must have seemed something grimmer to the home-bred lad than that mother-interpreted poverty, which he had hitherto known. But he met it full-face, bravely, uncomplainingly, and, best of all, with unfailing good humour. And the little alleviations which friends made in his hard lot were all received in a spirit of the sincerest, charmingest gratitude. He never took a kindness as ' his due '; never thought, like so many embryo geniuses, that his talents gave him right of toll on his richer brethren. ' Because I would drink at the well,' he would say in his picturesque fashion, ' am I to expect every one to haste and fill my cup from their pitchers? No, I must draw the water for myself, or I must go thirsty. I have no claim save my desire to learn, and what is that to others?' Thus he preserved his self-respect and his independence.

He worked hard, and, first of all, he wisely sought to free himself from all voluntary disabilities; there were enough and to spare of legally imposed ones to keep him mindful of his Judaism. He felt strong enough in faith to need no artificial shackles. He would be Jew, and yet German—patriot, but no pariah. He would eschew vague dreams of universalism, false ideas of tribalism. If Palestine had not been, he, its product, could not be; but Palestine and its glories were of the past and of the future; the present only was his, and he must shape his life according to its conditions, which placed him, in the eighteenth century, born of Jewish parents, in a German city. He was German by birth, Jew by descent and by conviction; he would fulfil all the obligations which country, race, and religion impose. But a German Jew, who did not speak the language of his country? That, surely, was an anomaly and must be set right. So he set himself strenuously to learn German, and to make it his native language. Such secular study was by no means an altogether safe proceeding.

Ignorance, as we have seen, was 'protected'
in those days by Jewish ecclesiastical authority.   Free trade in literature was sternly
prohibited, and a German grammar, or a Latin
or a Greek one, had, in sober truth, to run
a strict blockade.   One Jewish lad, it is
recorded on very tolerable authority, was
actually in the year 1746 expelled the city
of Berlin for no other offence than that of
being caught in the act of studying—one
chronicle, indeed, says, carrying—some such
proscribed volume.   Moses, however, was
more fortunate; he saved money enough to
buy his books, or made friends enough to
borrow them; and, we may conclude, found
nooks in which to hide them, and hours in
which to read them.   He set himself, too,
to gain some knowledge of the Classics, and
here he found a willing teacher in one Kish,
a medical student from Prague.   Later on,
another helper was gained in a certain Israel
Moses, a Polish schoolmaster, afterwards known
as Israel Samosc.   This man was a fine mathematician, and a first-rate Hebrew scholar;
but as his attainments did not include the
German language, he made Euclid known to
Moses through the medium of a Hebrew
translation.   Moses, in return, imparted to
Samosc his newly acquired German, and learnt
it, of course, more thoroughly through teach-

ing it. He must have possessed the art of making friends who were able to take on themselves the office of teachers; for presently we find him, in odd half-hours, studying French and English under a Dr. Aaron Emrich.[1] He very early began to make translations of parts of the Scripture into German, and these attempts indicate that, from the first, his overpowering desire for self-culture sprang from no selfishness. He wanted to open up the closed roads to place and honour, but not to tread them alone, not to leave his burdened brethren on the bye-paths, whilst he sped on rejoicing. He knew truly enough that 'the light was sweet,' and that 'a pleasant thing it is to behold the sun.' But he heeded, too, the other part of the charge: he 'remembered the days of darkness, which were many.' He remembered them always, heedfully, pitifully, patiently; and to the weary eyes which would not look up or could not, he ever strove to adjust the beautiful blessed light which he knew, and they, poor souls, doubted, was good. He never thrust it, unshaded, into their gloom: he never carried it off to illumine his own path.

Thus, the translations at which Moses

[1] Better known to scholars as Dr. Aaron Solomon Gompertz.

Mendelssohn worked were no transcripts from learned treatises which might have found a ready market among the scholars of the day; but unpaid and unpaying work from the liturgy and the Scriptures, done with the object that his people might by degrees share his knowledge of the vernacular, and become gradually aud unconsciously familiar with the language of their country through the only medium in which there was any likelihood of their studying it. With that one set purpose always before him, of drawing his people with him into the light, he presently formed the idea of issuing a serial in Hebrew, which, under the title of *The Moral Preacher*, should introduce short essays and transcripts on other than strictly Judaic or religious subjects. One Bock was his coadjutor in this project, and two numbers of the little work were published. The contents do not seem to have been very alarming. To our modern notions of periodical literature, they would probably be a trifle dull; but their mild philosophy and yet milder science proved more than enough to arouse the orthodox fears of the poor souls, who, 'bound in affliction and iron,' distrusted even the gentle hand which was so eager to loose the fetters. There was a murmur of doubt, of muttered dislike of 'strange customs'; perhaps here and there

too, a threat concerning the pains and penalties
which attached to the introduction of such.
At any rate, but two numbers of the poor
little reforming periodical appeared; and
Moses, not angry at his failure, not more than
momentarily discouraged by it, accepted the
position and wasted no time nor temper in
cavilling at it.   He had learnt to labour, he
could learn to wait.   And thus, in hard yet
happy work, passed away the seven years, from
fourteen till twenty-one, which are the seed-
time of a man's life.   In 1750, when Moses
was nearly of age, he came into possession of
what really proved an inheritance.   A rich
silk manufacturer, named Bernhardt, who was
a prominent member of the Berlin synagogue,
made a proposal to the learned young man,
whose perseverance had given reputation to
his scholarship, to become resident tutor to
his children.   The offer was gladly accepted,
and it may be considered Mendelssohn's first
step on the road to success.   The first step to
fame had been taken when the boy had set
out on his long tramp to Berlin.

Bernhardt was a kind and cultured man,
and in his house Mendelssohn found both congenial occupation and welcome leisure.   He
was teacher by day, studentby night, and
author at odd half-hours.   He turned to his
books with the greatest ardour; and we

read of him studying Locke and Plato in the original, for by this time English and Greek were both added to his store of languages. His pupils, meanwhile, were never neglected, nor in the pursuit of great ends were trifles ignored. In more than one biography special emphasis is laid on his beautifully neat handwriting, which, we are told, much excited his employer's admiration. This humble, but very useful, talent may possibly have been inherited, with some other small-sounding virtues, from the poor father in Dessau, to whom many a nice present was now frequently sent. At the end of three or four years of tutorship, Bernhardt's appreciation of the young man took a very practical expression. He offered Moses Mendelssohn the position of book-keeper in his factory, with some especial responsibilities and emoluments attached to the office. It was a splendid opening, although Moses Mendelssohn, the philosopher, eagerly and gratefully accepting such a post somehow jars on one's susceptibilities, and seems almost an instance of the round man pushed into the square hole. It was, however, an assured position; it gave him leisure, it gave him independence, and in due time wealth, for as years went on he grew to be a manager, and finally a partner in the house. His tastes had already drawn him into the outer literary circle of Berlin, which at this time had its headquarters in a sort of club, which met to play chess and to discuss politics and philosophy, and which numbered Dr. Gompertz, the promising young scholar Abbt, and Nicolai, the bookseller,[1] among its members. With these and other kindred spirits, Mendelssohn soon found pleasant welcome ; his talents and geniality quickly overcoming any social prejudices, which, indeed, seldom flourish in the republic of letters. And, early disadvantages notwithstanding, we may conclude without much positive evidence on the subject, that Mendelssohn possessed that valuable, indefinable gift, which culture, wealth, and birth united occasionally fail to bestow—the gift of good manners. He was free alike from conceit and dogmatism, the Scylla and Charybdis to most young men of exceptional talent. He had the loyal nature and the noble mind, which we are told on high authority is the necessary root of the rare flower ; and he had, too, the sympathetic, unselfish feeling which we are wont to summarise shortly as a good heart, and which is the first essential to good manners.

When Lessing came to Berlin, about 1745, his play of *Die Juden* was already published, and his reputation sufficiently established to make him an honoured guest at these little

---

[1] Later, the noted publisher of that name.

literary gatherings. Something of affinity in
the wide, unconventional, independent natures
of the two men; something, it may be, of likeness in unlikeness in their early struggles with
fate, speedily attracted Lessing and Mendelssohn to each other. The casual acquaintance soon ripened into an intimate and lifelong friendship, which gave to Mendelssohn,
the Jew, wider knowledge and illimitable
hopes of the outer, inhospitable world—which
gave to Lessing, the Christian, new belief in
long-denied virtues; and which, best of all,
gave to humanity those 'divine lessons of
Nathan der Weise,' as Goethe calls them—
for which character Mendelssohn sat, all unconsciously, as model, and scarcely idealised
model, to his friend. It was, most certainly,
a rarely happy friendship for both, and for
the world. Lessing was the godfather of
Mendelssohn's first book. The subject was
suggested in the course of conversation between them, and a few days after Mendelssohn brought his manuscript to Lessing.
He saw no more of it till his friend handed
him the proofs and a small sum for the copy-
right; and it was in this way that the
Philosophische Gespräche was anonymously
published in 1754. Later, the friends brought
out together a little book, entitled *Pope as
a Metaphysician*, and this was followed up

with some philosophical essays ('Briefe über die Empfindungen') which quickly ran through three editions, and Mendelssohn became known as an author. A year or two later, he gained the prize which the Royal Academy of Berlin offered for the best essay on the problem 'Are metaphysics susceptible of mathematical demonstration?' for which prize Kant was one of the competitors.

Lessing's migration to Leipzig, and his temporary absences from the capital in the capacity of tutor, made breaks, but no diminution, in the friendship with Mendelssohn; and the *Literatur-Briefe*, a journal cast in the form of correspondence on art, science, and literature, to which Nicolai, Abbt, and other writers were occasional contributors, continued its successful publication till the year 1765. A review in this journal of one of the literary efforts of Frederick the Second gave rise to a characteristic ebullition of what an old writer quaintly calls 'the German endemical distemper of Judæophobia.' In this essay, Mendelssohn had presumed to question some of the conclusions of the royal author; and although the contents of the *Literatur-Briefe* were generally unsigned, the anonymity was in most cases but a superficial disguise. The paper drew down upon Mendelssohn the denunciation of a too loyal

subject of Frederick's, and he was summoned
to Sans Souci to answer for it.   Frederick
appears to have been more sensible than his
thin-skinned defender, and the interview
passed off amicably enough.   Indeed, a short
while after, we hear of a petition being prepared to secure to Mendelssohn certain rights
and privileges of dwelling unmolested in
whichever quarter of the city he might choose
—a right which at that time was granted to
but few Jews, and at a goodly expenditure
of both capital and interest.   Mendelssohn,
loyal to his brethren, long and stoutly refused
to have any concession granted on the score
of his talents which he might not claim on
the score of his manhood in common with the
meanest and most ignorant of his co-religionists.   And there is some little doubt whether
the partial exemptions which Mendelssohn
subsequently obtained, were due to the petition, which suffered many delays and vicissi-
tudes in the course of presentation, or to the
subtle and silent force of public opinion.

Meanwhile Mendelssohn married, and the
story of his wooing, as first told by Berthold
Auerbach, makes a pretty variation on the
old theme.   It was, in this case, no short
idyll of 'she was beautiful and he fell in love.'
To begin with, it was all prosaic enough.   A
certain Abraham Gugenheim, a trader at

Hamburg, caused it to be hinted to Mendelssohn that he had a virtuous and blue-eyed but portionless daughter, named Fromet, who had heard of the philosopher's fame, and had read portions of his books; and who, mutual friends considered, would make him a careful and loving helpmate. So Mendelssohn, who was now thirty-two years old, and desirous to 'settle,' went to the merchant's house and saw the prim German maiden, and talked with her; and was pleased enough with her talk, or perhaps with the silent eloquence of the blue eyes, to go next day to the father and to say he thought Fromet would suit him for a wife. But to his surprise Gugenheim hesitated, and stiffness and embarrassment seemed to have taken the place of the yesterday's cordial greeting; still, it was no objection on *his* part, he managed at last to stammer out. For a minute Mendelssohn was hopelessly puzzled, but only for a minute; then it flashed upon him, 'It is she who objects!' he exclaimed; 'then it must be my hump'; and the poor father of course could only uncomfortably respond with apologetic platitudes about the unaccountability of girls' fancies. The humour as well as the pathos of the situation touched Mendelssohn, for he had no vanity to be piqued, and he instantly resolved to do his best to win this Senta-like maiden, who, less fortunate than the Dutch heroine, had had her pretty dreams of a hero dispelled, instead of accentuated by actual vision. Might he see her once again, he asked. 'To say farewell? Certainly!' answered the father, glad that his awkward mission was ending so amicably. So Mendelssohn went again, and found Fromet with the blue eyes bent steadily over her work; perhaps to hide a tear as much as to prevent a glance, for Fromet, as the sequel shows, was a tender-hearted maiden, and although she did not like to look at her deformed suitor, she did not want to wound him. Then Mendelssohn began to talk, beautiful glowing talk, and the spell which his writings had exercised began again to work on the girl. From philosophy to love, in its impersonal form, is an easy transition. She grew interested and self-forgetful. 'And do *you* think that marriages are made in heaven?' she eagerly questioned, as some early quaint superstition on this most attractive of themes was vividly touched upon by her visitor. 'Surely,' he replied; 'and some old beliefs on this head assert that all such contracts are settled in childhood. Strange to say, a special legend attaches itself to my fortune in this matter; and as our talk has led to this subject perhaps I may venture to tell it to you. The twin spirit which fate allotted to me, I am told, was fair, blue-eyed, and richly endowed with all spiritual charms; but, alas! ill-luck had added to her physical gifts a hump. A chorus of lamentation arose from the angels who minister in these matters. The "pity of it" was so evident. The burden of such a deformity might well outweigh all the other gifts of her beautiful youth, might render her morose, self-conscious, unhappy. If the load now had been but laid on a man! And the angels pondered, wondering, waiting to see if any would volunteer to take the maiden's burden from her. And I sprang up, and prayed that it might be laid upon my shoulders. And it was settled so.' There was a minute's pause, and then, so the story goes, the work was passionately thrown down, and the tender blue eyes were streaming, and the rest we may imagine. The simple, loving heart was won, and Fromet became his wife.

They had a modest little house with a pretty garden on the outskirts of Berlin, where a good deal of hospitality went on in a quiet, friendly way. The ornaments of their dwelling were, perhaps, a little disproportionate in size and quantity to the rest of the surroundings; but this was no matter of choice on the part of the newly married couple, since one of the minor

vexations imposed on Jews at this date was the
obligation laid on every bridegroom to treat
himself to a large quantity of china for the
good of the manufactory. The tastes or the
wants of the purchaser were not consulted;
and in this especial instance twenty life-sized
china apes were allotted to the bridegroom.
We may imagine poor Mendelssohn and his
wife eyeing these apes often, somewhat as
Cinderella looked at her pumpkin when
longing for the fairy's transforming wand.
Possibilities of those big baboons changed into
big books may have tantalised Mendelssohn;
whilst Fromet's more prosaic mind may have
confined itself to china and yet have found an
unlimited range for wishing. However, the
unchanged and unchanging apes notwithstanding, Mendelssohn and his wife enjoyed very
many years of quiet and contented happiness,
and by and by came children, four of them,
and then those old ungainly grievances were,
it is likely, transformed into playfellows.

Parenthood, perhaps, is never quite easy, but
it was a very difficult duty, and a terribly divided
one, for a cultivated man who a century ago
desired to bring up his children as good Jews
and good citizens. Many a time, it stands on
record, when this patient, self-respecting, un-
offending scholar took his children for a walk
coarse epithets and insulting cries followed

them through the streets. No resentment was politic, no redress was possible. ' Father, is it *wicked* to be a Jew ? ' his children would ask, as time after time the crowd hooted at them. ' Father, is it *good* to be a Jew ? ' they grew to ask later on, when in more serious walks of life they found all gates but the Jews' gate closed against them. Mendelssohn must have found such questions increasingly difficult to answer or to parry. Their very talents, which enlarged the boundaries, must have made his clever children rebel against the limitations which were so cruelly imposed. His eldest son Joseph early developed a strong scientific bias ; how could this be utilised ? The only profession which he, as a Jew, might enter, was that of medicine, and for that he had a decided distaste : perforce he was sent to commercial pursuits, and his especial talent had to run to waste, or, at best, to dilettantism. When this Joseph had sons of his own, can we wonder very much that he cut the knot and saved his children from a like experience, by bringing them up as Christians ?

Mendelssohn himself, all his life through, was unswervingly loyal to his faith. He took every disability accruing from it, as he took his own especial one, as being, so far as he was concerned, inevitable, and thus to be borne as patiently as might be. To him, most certainly, it would never have occurred to slip from under a burden which had been laid upon him to bear.   Concerning Fromet's influence on her children records are silent, and we are driven to conjecture that the pretty significance of her name was somewhat meaningless.[1]   The story of her wooing suggests susceptibility, perhaps, rather than strength of heart; and it may be that as years went on the 'blue eyes' got into a habit of weeping only over sorrows and wrongs which needed a less eloquent and a more helpful mode of treatment.

If Mendelssohn's wife had been able to show her children the home side of Jewish life, its suggestive ceremonialism, its domestic compensations—possibly her sons, almost certainly her daughters, would have learnt the brave, sweet patience that was common to Jewish mothers.   But this takes us to the region of 'might have been.'   Gentle, tender-hearted Fromet, it is to be feared, failed in true piety, and, the mother anchor missing, the children drifted from their moorings.

The leisure of the years succeeding his marriage was fully occupied by Mendelssohn in literary pursuits.   The whole of the Pentateuch was, by degrees, translated into pure

---

[1] Fromet was the affectionate diminutive of *Fromm* —pious.   Pet names of this sort were common at that time; we often come across a Gütle or Schönste or the like.

German, and simultaneous editions were published in German and in Hebrew characters. This great gift to his people was followed by a metrical translation of the Psalms; a work which took him ten years, during which time he always carried about with him a Hebrew Psalter, interleaved with blank pages. In 1783 he published his *Jerusalem*,[1] a sort of Church and State survey of the Jewish religion. The first and larger part of it dwells on the distinction between Judaism, as a State religion, and Judaism as the 'inheritance' of a dispersed nationality. He essays to prove the essential differences between civil and religious government, and to demonstrate that penal enactments, which in the one case were just and defensible, were, in the changed circumstances of the other, harmful, and, in point of fact, unjudicial. The work was, in effect, a masterly effort on Mendelssohn's part to exorcise the 'cursing spirit' which, engendered partly by long-suffered persecution, and partly by long association with the strict discipline of the Catholic Church, had taken a firm grip on Jewish ecclesiastical authority, and was constantly expressing itself in bitter anathema and morose excommunication. The second part of the book is mainly concerned with a vindication of the Jewish character and a plea

[1] *Jerusalem, oder über religiöse Macht und Judenthum.*

for toleration. Scholarly and temperate as is
the tone of this work throughout, it yet evoked
a good deal of rough criticism from the so-
called orthodox in both religious camps—from
those well-meaning, purblind persons of the
sort who, Lessing declares, see only one road,
and strenuously deny the possible existence of
any other.

In 1777, Frederic the Second desired to
judge for himself whether Jewish ecclesiastical
authority clashed at any point with the State or
municipal law of the land. A digest of the
Jewish Code on the general questions, and
more especially on the subject of property and
inheritance, was decreed to be prepared in
German, and to Mendelssohn was intrusted
the task. He had the assistance of the Chief
Rabbi of Berlin, and the result of these
labours was published in 1778, under the title
of *Ritual Laws of the Jews*. Another Jewish
philosophical work (published in 1785) was
Morning Hours.[1] This was a volume of essays
on the evidences of the existence of the Deity
and of conclusions concerning His attributes
deduced from the contemplation of His works.
Originally these essays had been given in the
form of familiar lectures on natural philosophy
by Mendelssohn to his children and to one or

---

[1] *Morgenstunden, oder Vorlesungen über das Daseyn
Gottes.*

two of their friends (including the two Humboldts) in his own house, every morning. In the same category of more distinctively Jewish books we may place a translation of Manasseh Ben Israel's famous *Vindiciæ Judæorum*, which he published, with a very eloquent preface, so early as 1781, just at the time when Dohm's generous work on the condition of the Jews as citizens of the State had made its auspicious appearance. Although this is one of Mendelssohn's minor efforts, the preface contains many a beautiful passage. His gratitude to Dohm is so deep and yet so dignified; his defence of his people is so wide, and his belief in humanity so sincere; and the whole is withal so short, that it makes most pleasant reading. One small quotation may perhaps be permitted, as pertinent to some recent discussions on Jewish subjects. 'It is,' says he, 'objected by some that the Jews are both too indolent for agriculture and too proud for mechanical trades; that if the restrictions were removed they would uniformly select the arts and sciences, as less laborious and more profitable, and soon engross all light, genteel, and learned professions. But those who thus argue conclude from the *present* state of things how they will be in the *future*, which is not a fair mode of reasoning. What should induce a Jew to waste his time in learning to manage the plough, the trowel, the plane, etc., while he knows he can make no practical use of them? But put them in his hand and suffer him to follow the bent of his inclinations as freely as other subjects of the State, and the result will not long be doubtful.   Men of genius and talent will, of course, embrace the learned professions; those of inferior capacity will turn their minds to mechanical pursuits; the rustic will cultivate the land; each will contribute, according to his station in life, his quota to the aggregate of productive labour.'

As he says in some other place of himself, nature never intended him, either physically or morally, for a wrestler; and this little essay, where there is no strain of argument or scope for deep erudition, is yet no unworthy specimen of the great philosopher's powers.   Poetic attempts too, and mostly on religious subjects, occasionally varied his counting-house duties and his more serious labours; but although he truly possessed, if ever man did, what Landor calls 'the poetic heart,' yet it is in his prose, rather than in his poetry, that we mostly see its evidences.   The book which is justly claimed as his greatest, and which first gave him his title to be considered a wide and deep-thinking philosopher, is his *Phædon*.[1] The idea of such a work had long been

---

[1] *Phædon, oder über die Unsterblichkeit der Seele.*

germinating in him, and the death of his dear friend Abbt, with whom he had had many a fruitful discussion on the subject, turned his thoughts more fixedly on the hopes which make sorrows bearable, and the work was published in the year following Abbt's death.

The first part is a very pure and classical German rendering of the original Greek form of Plato, and the remainder an eloquent summary of all that religion, reason, and experience urge in support of a belief in immortality. It is cast in the form of conversation between Socrates and his friends—a choice in composition which caused a Jewish critic (M. David Friedländer) to liken Moses Mendelssohn to Moses the lawgiver. 'For Moses spake, and *Socrates* was to him as a mouth' (Ex. iv. 15). In less than two years *Phædon* ran through three German editions, and it was speedily translated into English, French, Dutch, Italian, Danish, and Hebrew. Then, at one stride, came fame ; and great scholars, great potentates, and even the heads of his own community, sought his society. But fame was ever of incomparably less value to Mendelssohn than friendship, and any sort of notoriety he honestly hated. Thus, when his celebrity brought upon him a polemical discussion, the publicity which ensued, notwithstanding that the personal honour in

which he was held was thereby enhanced, so
thoroughly upset his nerves that the result
was a severe and protracted illness.   It came
about in this wise: Lavater, the French
pastor, in 1769, had translated Bonnet's
Evidences of Christianity into German; he
published it with the following dedication to
Moses Mendelssohn :—

'DEAR SIR,—I think I cannot give you a
stronger proof of my admiration of your excellent writings, and of your still more excellent
character, that of an Israelite in whom there
is no guile; nor offer you a better requital for
the great gratification which I, some years
ago, enjoyed in your interesting society, than
by dedicating to you the ablest philosophical
inquiry into the evidences of Christianity that
I am acquainted with.

'I am fully conscious of your profound
judgment, steadfast love of truth, literary
independence, enthusiasm for philosophy in
general, and esteem for Bonnet's works in
particular.   The amiable discretion with
which, notwithstanding your contrariety to
the Christian religion, you delivered your
opinion on it, is still fresh in my memory.
And so indelible and important is the impression which your truly philosophical respect
for the moral character of its Founder made

on me, in one of the happiest moments
of my existence, that I venture to beseech
you—nay, before the God of Truth, your and
my Creator and Father, I beseech and conjure
you—to read this work, I will not say with
philosophical impartiality, which I am confi-
dent will be the case, but for the purpose of
publicly refuting it, in case you should find
the main arguments, in support of the facts
of Christianity, untenable; or should you find
them conclusive, with the determination of
doing what policy, love of truth, and probity
demand—what Socrates would doubtless have
done had he read the work and found it un-
answerable.

'May God still cause much truth and virtue
to be disseminated by your means, and make
you experience the happiness my whole heart
wishes you.   JOHANN CASPAR LAVATER.

'ZURICH, *25th of August* 1769.'

It was a most unpleasant position for
Mendelssohn. Plain speaking was not so
much the fashion then as now, and defence
might more easily be read as defiance. At
that time the position of the Jews in all the
European States was most precarious, and
outspoken utterances might not only alienate
the timid followers whom Mendelssohn hoped
to enlighten, but probably offend the power-

ful outsiders whom he was beginning to influence. No man has any possible right to demand of another a public confession of faith; the conversation to which Lavater alluded as some justification for his request had been a private one, and the reference to it, moreover, was not altogether accurate. And Mendelssohn hated controversy, and held a very earnest conviction that no good cause, certainly no religious one, is ever much forwarded by it. Should he be silent, refuse to reply, and let judgment go by default? Comfort and expediency both pleaded in favour of this course, but truth was mightier and prevailed. Like unto the three who would not be 'careful' of their answer even under the ordeal of fire, he soon decided to testify plainly and without undue thought of consequences. Mendelssohn was not the sort to serve God with special reservations as to Rimmon. Definitely he answered his too zealous questioner in a document which is so entirely full of dignity and of reason that it is difficult to make quotations from it.[1] 'Certain inquiries,' he writes, 'we finish once for all in our lives.' . . . 'And I herewith declare in the presence of the God of truth, your and my Creator, by whom you have conjured me in

[1] The whole correspondence can be read in *Memoirs of Moses Mendelssohn*, by M. Samuels, published in 1827.

your dedication, that I will adhere to my principles so long as my entire soul does not assume another nature.' And then, emphasising the position that it is by character and not by controversy that *he* would have Jews shame their traducers, he goes fully and boldly into the whole question. He shows with a delicate touch of humour that Judaism, in being no proselytising faith, has a claim to be let alone. ' I am so fortunate as to count amongst my friends many a worthy man who is not of my faith. Never yet has my heart whispered, Alas! for this good man's soul. He who believes that no salvation is to be found out of the pale of his own church, must often feel such sighs arise in his bosom.' 'Suppose there were among my contemporaries a Confucius or a Solon, I could consistently with my religious principles love and admire the great man, but I should never hit on the idea of converting a Confucius or a Solon. What should I convert him for ? As he does not belong to the congregation of Jacob, my religious laws were not made for him, and on doctrines we should soon come to an understanding. Do I think there is a chance of his being saved ? I certainly believe that he who leads mankind on to virtue in this world cannot be damned in the next.' 'We believe . . . that those who regulate their lives according to the religion of nature and

of reason are called virtuous men of other
nations, and are, equally with our patriarchs, the
children of eternal salvation.' 'Whoever is not
born conformable to our laws has no occasion
to live according to them. We alone consider
ourselves bound to acknowledge their authority,
and this can give no offence to our neighbours.'
He refuses to criticise Bonnet's work in detail
on the ground that in his opinion 'Jews should
be scrupulous in abstaining from reflections on
the predominant religion'; but nevertheless,
whilst repeating his 'so earnest wish to have
no more to do with religious controversy,' the
honesty of the man asserts itself in boldly
adding, 'I give you at the same time to understand that I could, very easily, bring forward
something in refutation of M. Bonnet's work.'

Mendelssohn's reply brought speedily, as it
could scarcely fail to do, an ample and sincere
apology from Lavater, a 'retracting' of the
challenge, an earnest entreaty to forgive what
had been 'importunate and improper' in the
dedicator, and an expression of 'sincerest
respect' and 'tenderest affection' for his
correspondent. Mendelssohn's was a nature
to have more sympathy with the errors inci-
dental to too much, than to too little zeal, and
the apology was accepted as generously as it
was offered. And here ended, so far as the
principals were concerned, this somewhat

unique specimen of a literary squabble. A crowd of lesser writers, unfortunately, hastened to make capital out of it; and a bewildering mist of nondescript and pedantic compositions soon darkened the literary firmament, obscuring and vulgarising the whole subject. They took 'sides' and gave 'views' of the controversy; but Mendelssohn answered none and read as few as possible of these publications. Still the strain and worry told on his sensitive and peace-loving nature, and he did not readily recover his old elasticity of temperament.

In 1778 Lessing's wife died, and his friend's trouble touched deep chords both of sympathy and of memory in Mendelssohn. Yet more cruelly were they jarred when, two years later, Lessing himself followed, and an uninterrupted friendship of over thirty years was thus dissolved. Lessing and Mendelssohn had been to each other the sober realisation of the beautiful ideal embodied in the drama of *Nathan der Weise*. 'What to you makes me seem Christian makes of you the Jew to me,' each could most truly say to the other. They helped the world to see it too, and to recognise the Divine truth that 'to be to the best thou knowest ever true is all the creed.'

The death of his friend was a terrible blow to Mendelssohn. 'After wrinkles come,' says Mr. Lowell, in likening ancient friendships to slow-growing trees, 'few plant, but water dead ones with vain tears.' In this case, the actual pain of loss was greatly aggravated by some publications which appeared shortly after Lessing's death, impugning his sincerity and religious feeling. Germany, as Goethe once bitterly remarked, 'needs time to be thankful.' In the first year or two following Lessing's death it was, perhaps, too early to expect gratitude from his country for the lustre his talents had shed on it. Some of the pamphlets would make it seem that it was too early even for decency. Mendelssohn vigorously took up the cudgels for his dead friend; too vigorously, perhaps, since Kant remarked that 'it is Mendelssohn's fault, if Jacobi (the most notorious of the assailants) should now consider himself a philosopher.' To Mendelssohn's warm-hearted, generous nature it would, however, have been impossible to remain silent when one whom he knew to be tolerant, earnest, and sincere in the fullest sense of those words of highest praise, was accused of 'covert Spinozism'; a charge which again was broadly rendered, by these wretched, ignorant interpreters of a language they failed to understand, as atheism and hypocrisy.

But this was his last literary work. It shows no sign of decaying powers; it is full of pathos, of wit, of clear close reasoning, and of brilliant satire; yet nevertheless it was his monument as well as his friend's. He took the manuscript to his publisher in the last day of the year 1785; and in the first week of the New Year 1786, still only fifty-six years old, he quietly and painlessly died. That last work seems to make a beautiful and fitting end to his life; a life which truly adds a worthy stanza to what Herder calls 'the greatest poem of all time—the history of the Jews.'

THE NATIONAL IDEA IN JUDAISM

ONCE find a man's ideals, it has been well said, and the rest is easy; and undoubtedly to get at any true notion of character, one must discover these. They may be covered close with conventionalities, or jealously hidden, like buried treasures, from unsympathetic eyes; but the patient search is well worth while, since it is his ideals—and not his words nor his deeds, which a thousand circumstances influence and decide—which show us the real man as known to his Maker. And true as this is of the individual, it is true in a deeper and larger sense of the nations, and most true of all of that people with whom for centuries speech was impolitic and action impossible. With articulate expression so long denied to them, the national ideals must be always to the student of history the truest revelation of Judaism; and it is curious and interesting to trace their development, and to recognise the crown and apex of them all in battlefield and in 'Vineyard,' in Ghetto and in mart, unchanged among the changes, and practically the same as in the days of the desert. The germ was set in the wilderness, when, amid the thunders and lightnings of Sinai, a crowd of frightened, freshly rescued slaves were made 'witnesses' to a living God, and guardians of a 'Law' which demonstrated His existence. Very new and strange, and but dimly understanded of the people it must all have been. 'The lights of sunset and of sunrise mixed.' The fierce vivid glow under which they had bent and basked in Egypt had scarcely faded, when they were bid look up in the grey dawn of the desert to receive their trust. There was worthy stuff in the descendants of the man who had left father and friends and easy, sensuous idolatry to follow after an ideal of righteousness; and they who had but just escaped from the bondage of centuries, rose to the occasion. They accepted their mission; 'All that the Lord has spoken will we do,' came up a responsive cry from 'all the people answering together,' and in that supreme moment the ill-fed and so recently ill-treated groups were transformed into a nation. 'I will make of thee a great people'; 'Through thee shall all families of the earth be blessed'; the meaning of such predictions was borne in upon them in one bewildering flash, and in that flash the national idea of Judaism

found its dawn; they, the despised and the
downtrodden, were to become trustees of
civilisation.

As the glow died down, however, a very
rudimentary sort of civilisation the wilderness
must have presented to these builders of the
temples and the treasure cities by the Nile,
and to the vigorous, resourceful Hebrew
women. As day after day, and year after
year, the cloud moved onward, darkening the
road which it directed, as they gathered the
manna and longed for the fleshpots, it could
have been only the few and finer spirits among
those listless groups who were able to discern
that a civilisation based upon the Decalogue,
shorn though it was of all present pleasantness
and ease, had a promise about it that was
lacking to a culture, ' learned in all the wisdom
of the Egyptians.' It was life reduced to its
elements ; Sinai and Pisgah stood so far apart,
and such long level stretches of dull sand lay
between the heights. One imagines the
women, skilled like their men-folk in all
manner of cunning workmanship, eagerly,
generously ransacking their stores of purple
and fine linen to decorate the Tabernacle, and
spinning and embroidering with a desperately
delighted sense of recovered refinements,
which, as much perhaps as their fervour of
religious enthusiasm, led them to bring their

gifts till restrained 'from bringing.' The trust was accepted though in the wilderness, but grudgingly, with many a faint-hearted protest, and to some minds, in some moods, slavery must have seemed less insistent in its demands than trusteeship.

The conquest of Canaan was the next experience, and as sinfulness and idolatry were relentlessly washed away in rivers of blood, one doubts if the impressionable descendants of Jacob, to whom it was given to overcome, might not perchance have preferred to endure. But such choice was not given to them; the trust had to be realised before it could be transmitted, and its value tested by its cost. With Palestine at last in possession of the chosen people, this civilisation of which they were the guardians by slow degrees became manifest. Samuel lived it, and David sang it, and Isaiah preached it, and the nation clung to it, individual men and women, stumbling and failing often, but dying each, when need came, a hundred deaths in its defence; perhaps finding it on occasion less difficult to die for an idea than to live up to it.

The securities were shifted, the terms of the trusteeship changed when the people of the Land became the people of the Book. The civilisation which they guarded grew narrower in its issues and more limited in its outlook, till, as the years rolled into the centuries, it was hard to recognise the 'witnesses' of God in the hunted outcasts of man. Yet to the student of history, who reads the hieroglyph of the Egyptian into the postcard of to-day, it is not difficult to see the civilisation of Sinai shining under the folds of the gaberdine or of the *san benito*. It was taught in the schools and it was lived in the homes, and the Ghetto could not altogether degrade it, nor the Holy Office effectually disguise it. Jews sank sometimes to the lower level of the sad lives they led, but Judaism remained unconquerably buoyant. Judaism, as they believed in it, was a Personal Force making for righteousness, a Law which knew no change, the Promise of a period when the earth should be filled with the knowledge of the Lord; and the 'witnesses' stuck to this their trust, through good repute and through evil repute, with a simple doggedness which disarms all superficial criticism. The glamour of the cause, through which a Barcochba could loom heroic to an Akiba, the utter absence of self-consciousness or of self-seeking, which made Judas in his fight for freedom pin the Lord's name on his flag, and which, with the kingdom lost, made the scrolls of the Law the spoil with which Ben Zaccai retreated—this was at the root of the national idea, and its impersonality gives the secret of its strength,

'Not unto us, O Lord, not unto us, but unto Thy name!' This vivid sense of being the trustees of civilisation was wholly dissociated from any feeling of conceit either in the leaders or in the rank and file of the Jewish nation. It is curious indeed to realise how so intense a conviction of the survival of the fittest could be held in so intensely unmodernised a spirit.

The idea of their trusteeship was a sheet anchor to the Jews as the waves and the billows passed over them. In the fifteen hundred years' tragedy of their history there have been no *entr'actes* of frenzied stampede or of revolutionary, revengeful conspiracy. A resolute endurance, which, characteristically enough, rarely approaches asceticism, marks the depth and strength and buoyancy of the national idea. Trustees of civilisation might not sigh nor sing in solitudes; nor with the feeling so keen that 'a thousand years in Thy sight are but as a day,' was it worth while to plot or plan against the oppressors of the moment. Time was on their side, and 'that which shapes it to some perfect end.' And this attitude explains, possibly, some unattractive phases of it, since however honestly the individual consciousness may be absorbed in a national conscience, yet the individual will generally, in some way, manage to express himself, and the self is not always quite up to the ideal, nor indeed is it always in harmony with those who would interpret it. When a David dances before the Ark it needs other than a daughter of Saul to understand him. There have been Jews in David's case, their enthusiasm mocked at; and there have been Jews indifferent to their trust, and Jews who have betrayed it, and Jews too, and these not a few, who have pushed it into prominence with undue display. The infinite changes of circumstance and surrounding in Jewish fortunes no less than differences in individual character have induced a considerable divergence in the practical politics of the national idea. The persecuted have been exclusive over it, and the prosperous careless; it has been vulgarised by superstition, and ignored by indifferentism, till modern 'rational' thinkers now and again question whether Palestine be indeed the goal of Jewish separateness, and make it a matter for academic discussion whether 'Jews' mean a sect of cosmopolitan citizens with religious customs more or less in common, or a people whose religion has a national origin and a national purpose in its observances. With questioners such as these, Revelation, possibly, would not be admitted as sound evidence in reply, else the promise, 'Ye shall be to me a kingdom of priests and a holy nation,' would,

one might think, show a design that ritual by
itself does not fulfil.   It was no sect with
'tribal' customs, but a 'nation' and a 'kingdom' who were to be 'holy to the Lord.'   But
though texts may be inadmissible with those
who prefer their sermons in stones, yet the
records of the ages are little less impartial and
unimpassioned than the records of the rocks,
and doubters might find an answer in the insistent tones of history when she tells of the
results of occasional unnatural divorce between
religion and nationality among Jews.

There were times not a few, whilst their
own judges ruled, and whilst their own kings
reigned in Palestine, when, with a firm grip
on the land, but a loose hold on the law, Israel
was well-nigh lost and absorbed in the idola-
trous peoples by whom it was surrounded;
when the race, which was ceasing to worship
at the national altars, was in danger of ceasing
to exist as a nation.   Exile taught them to
value by loss what was possession.   'How shall
we sing the Lord's song in a strange land?'
was the passionate cry in Babylon.   Was it perchance the feeling that the land was 'strange,'
which gave that new fervour to the songs,
choking off utterance and finding adequate
expression only in the Return?   Did Judas,
the Maccabee, understand something of this
as he led his patriotic, 'zealous' troops to

victory? Did Mendelssohn forget it when, nineteen hundred years later, he emancipated his people from the results of worse than Syrian oppression, at the cost of so many, his own children among the rest, shaking off memories and duties as lightly as they shook off restraints? Over and over again, in the wonderful history of the Jews, does religion without nationality prove itself as impossible as nationality without religion to serve for a sustaining force in Judaism. The people who, while 'the city of palm-trees' was yet their own, could set up strange gods in the groves, were not one whit more false to their faith, nor more harmful to their people, than those later representatives of the opposite type, Hellenists, as history calls them, who built a temple, and read the law and observed the precepts, whilst their very priests changed their good Jewish names for Greek-sounding ones in contemptuous and contemptible depreciation of their Jewish nationality. One inclines, perhaps, to accentuate the facts of history and to moralise over the might-have-beens where these fit into a theory; but so much as this at least seems indisputable—that those who would dissociate the national from the religious, or the religious from the national element in Judaism attempt the impossible. The ideal of the Jews must always be 'from Zion shall come forth instruction, and the Word

of God from Jerusalem'; and to this end—
'that all people of the earth may know Thy
name, as do thy people Israel.' This is the
goal of Jewish separateness. The separateness may have been part of the Divine plan,
as distinctive practices and customs are due in
the first place to the Divine command; but
they are also and none the less a means of
strengthening the national character of the
Jews. Jewish religion neither 'happens'
to have a national origin, nor does Jewish
nationality 'happen' to have religious customs.
The Jewish nation has become a nation and
has been preserved as a nation for the distinct
purpose of religion. This, as we read it, is the
lesson of history. And this too is its consolation. The faithful few who see the fulfilment
of history and of prophecy in a restored and
localised nationality—a Jerusalem reinstated
as the joy of the whole earth; the careless
many who, in comfortable complacency, are
well content to await it indefinitely, in dispersion; the loyal many, who believe that a
political restoration would be a retrogressive
step, narrowing and embarrassing the wider
issues; the children of light and the children
of the world, the spiritual and the *spirituel*
element in Israel, alike, if unequally, have each
their share in spreading the civilisation of
Sinai, as surely as 'fire and hail and snow and

mist and stormy wind' all 'fulfil His word.'
The seed that was sown in the sands of the
desert has germinated through the ages, and
its fruition is foretold. The promise to the
Patriarch, ' I will make of thee a great nation,'
foreshadowed that his descendants were to be
trustees, ' through them shall all families of the
earth be blessed.' There are those who would
read into this national idea a taint of arrogance
or of exclusiveness, as there are some scientifi-
cally-minded folks, a trifle slow perhaps, to
apply their own favoured dogma of evolution,
who can see in the Exodus only a capriciously
selected band of slaves, led forth to serve a
tribal deity. But the history of the Jews,
which is inseparable from the religion of the
Jews, rebukes those who would thus halt mid-
way and stumble over the evidences. It lifts
the veil, it flashes the light on dark places, it
unriddles the weary puzzle of the travailing
ages, leaving only indifferentism unsolvable, as
it shows clear how the Lord, the Spirit of all
flesh, the universal Father, brought Israel out
of Egypt and gave them name and place to
be His witnesses, and the means He chose
whereby ' all families of the earth should be
blessed.'

THE STORY OF A FALSE PROPHET

EACH age has its illusions—illusions which succeeding ages with a recovered sense of sanity are often apt to record as the most incomprehensible of crazes. 'That poor will-o'-the-wisp mistaken for a shining light! Oh, purblind race of miserable men!' is the quick, contemptuous comment of a later, clearer-sighted generation. But one may question if such comment be always just. May not the narrow vision, too unseeing to be deceived, betoken a yet more hopeless sort of blindness than the wide-eyed gaze which, fixed on stars, blunders into quagmires? 'Where there is no vision,' it is written, 'the people perish'; and though stars may prove mirage and quagmires clinging mud, yet a long rank of shabby, shadowy heroes, who, more or less wittingly, have had the hard fate to lead a multitude to destruction, seems to suggest that such deluded multitudes are no dumb, driven cattle, but, capable of being led astray, have also the faculty of being led into the light. And if this, to our consolation, be the teaching of

history anent those whom it impartially dubs
impostors, then wasted loves and wasted beliefs
lose something of their hopeless sadness, and
in the transfiguration even failures and false
prophets are seen to have a place and use.

No more typical instance could be found of
the heights and depths of a people's power
of illusion—and that people one which in its
modern development might be lightly held
proof against most illusions—than the suggestive career of a Messiah of the seventeenth
century supplies to us.   Undying hope, it has
been said, is the secret of vision.   When hope
is dead the vision perchance takes unto itself
the awful condition of death, corruption, for
thus only could it have come to pass that that
same people, which had given an Isaiah to
the world, under the stress of inexorable
and inevitable circumstance brought forth a
Sabbathai Zevi.

'Of all mortal woes,' so declared the weeping Persian to Thersander at the banquet,
'the greatest is this : with many thoughts and
wise, to have no power.'   Under the crushing
burden of that mortal woe the Jewish race
had rested restlessly for over sixteen weary
centuries.   Power had passed from the dispossessed people with the fall of their
garrisoned Temple, and under dispersion and
persecution their 'many thoughts and wise'

had grown dumb, or shrill, or cruelly inarticulate. The kingdom of priests and the
kinsmen of the Maccabees had dwindled to
a community of pedants and pedlars. Into
the schools of the prophets had crept the
casuistries and subtleties of the Kabbalists;
and descendants of those who had been skilful
in all manner of workmanship now haggled
over wares which they lacked skill or energy
to produce. East and west the doom of
Herodotus was drearily apparent, and to an
onlooker it must have seemed incredible that
these poor pariahs, content to be contemned,
were of the same race which had sung the
Lord's songs and had fought the Lord's
battles. In the seventeenth century the fires
of the Inquisition were still smouldering, and
Jewish victims of the Holy Office, naked
and charred, or swathed and unrecognisable,
were fleeing hither and thither from its flames,
across the inhospitable continent of Europe.
Nearer to the old scenes was no nearer to
happiness; the farthest removed indeed from
any present realisation of ancient prosperity
seemed those wanderers who had turned their
tired, sad faces to the East. The land on
which Moses had looked from Pisgah; for
which, remembering Zion, the exiles in Babylon had wept; for which a later generation,
as unaided as undaunted, had fought and

died—this land, their heritage, had passed utterly from the possession of the Jews. 'Thou waterest its ridges: Thou settlest the furrows thereof.' Seemingly out of that ownership too the land had passed, for His ridges had run red with blood, and in His furrows the Romans had sown salt. From the very first century after Christ, Jews had been grudged a foothold in Judæa, and from the date of the Crusades any dwelling-place in their own land was definitely denied to the outcast race. A new meaning had been read into that ancient phrase, ' the joy of the whole earth.' The Holy City had come, in cruel, narrow limitation, to mean to its conquerors the Holy Sepulchre, all other of its memories ' but a dream and a forgetting.' And now, although the fervour of the Crusades had died away, and the stone stood at the mouth of the Sepulchre as undisturbed and almost as un-heeded of the outside world as when the two Marys kept their lonely vigil, yet enough still of all that terribly wasted wealth of enthusiasm survived to make the Holy Land difficult even of approach to its former rulers. Through all those centuries, for over sixteen hundred slow, sad, stormy years, this powerless people had borne their weary burden, ' the greatest of all mortal woes.' Occasionally, for a moment as it were, the passions of repulsed patriotism and of pent-up humanity would break bounds, and seek expression in a form which scholars could scarce interpret or priests control. With their law grudged to them and their land denied, 'their many thoughts and wise,' under cruel restraint, were dwindling into impotent dreams or flashing out in wild unlikeness of wisdom.

It was in the summer of the year 1666 that some such incomprehensible craze seemed to possess the ancient city of Smyrna. The sleepy stillness of the narrow streets was jarred by a thousand confused and unaccustomed sounds. The slow, smooth current of Eastern life seemed of a sudden stirred into a whirl of excited eddies. Men and women in swift-changing groups were sobbing, praying, laughing in a breath, their quick gesticulations in curious contrast with their sober, shabby garments, and their patient, pathetic eyes. And strangest thing of all, it was on a prophet in his own country, in the very city of his birth, that this extraordinary enthusiasm of greeting was being expended, and the name of the prophet was Sabbathai, son of Mordecai. Mordecai Zevi, the father, had dwelt among these townsfolk of Smyrna, dealing in money and dying of gout, and Sabbathai Zevi, the son, had been brought up among them, and not so many years since had been banished by them. In that passionately absorbed crowd there must have been many a middle-aged man old enough to remember how this turbulent son of the commonplace old broker had been sent forth from the city, and the gates shut on him in anger and contempt; and some there surely must have been who knew of his subsequent career. But if it were so, there were none sane enough to deduce a moral. It was in the character of Messiah and Deliverer that Sabbathai had come back to Smyrna, and long-dead hope, quickened into life at the very words, was strong enough to strangle a whole host of resistant memories, though, in truth, there was a great deal to forget. It had been at the instance of the religious authorities of the place, whose susceptibilities were shocked by the utterance of opinions advanced enough to provoke a tumult in the synagogue, that the young man had been expelled from the city. To young and ardent spirits in that crowd it is possible that this early experience of Sabbathai bore a very colourable imitation of martyrdom, and the life in exile that followed it may have appealed to their imaginations as the most fitting of preparations for a prophet. But then unfortunately Sabbathai's life in exile had not been that of a hermit, nor altogether of a sort to fit into any exalted theories. Au-

thentic news had certainly come of him as
a traveller in the Morea and in Syria, and
rumours had been rife concerning travelling
companions. Three successive marriages, it
was said, had taken place, followed in each
instance by unedifying quarrels and divorce.
Of the ladies little was known ; but it came to
be generally affirmed, on what, if sifted, perhaps
amounted to insufficient evidence, that each
wife was more marvellously handsome than
her predecessor. And then, for a while, these
lingering distorted sounds from the outside
world had died out in the sordid stillness of
their lives, to rise again suddenly, after long
interval, in startling echoes. The wildest of
rumours was all at once in the air, heralding
this much-married, banished disputant of the
synagogue, this turbulent, troublesome Sabbathai, as Messiah of the Jews. What he had
done, what he would do, what he could do,
was repeated from mouth to mouth with an
ever-growing exactness of exaggeration which
modern methods of transmitting news could
hardly surpass. One soberly circumstantial
tale was of a ship cruising off the north coast
of Scotland (of all places in the world !),
with sail and cordage of purest silk, her
ensign the Twelve Tribes, and her crew,
consistently enough, speaking Hebrew. A
larger and certainly more geographically

minded contingent of converts was said to be marching across the deserts of Arabia to proclaim the millennium. This host was identified as the lost Ten Tribes, and Sabbathai, mounted on a celestial lion with a bridle of serpents, was, or was shortly to be—for the reports were sometimes a little conflicting—at the head of this imposing multitude, and about to inaugurate a new and glorious Temple, which, all ready built and beautified, would straightway descend from heaven, and in which the services were likely to become popular, since all fasts were forthwith to be changed into festivals.

The rumours, it must be confessed, were all of a terribly materialistic sort, and one wonders somewhat sadly over Sabbathai's proclamation, questioning if the promise of 'dominion over the nations,' or the permission 'to do every day what is usual for you to do only on new moons,' roused most of the long-repressed human nature in those weary pariahs, the 'nation of the Jews,' to whom it was roundly addressed. All the cities of Turkey, an old chronicler tells us, 'were full of expectation.' Business in many places was altogether suspended. The belief in a reign of miracle was extended to daily needs, and trust in such needs being somehow supplied was esteemed as an essential test of general faith in the new order of things.　So none laboured, but all prayed, and purified themselves, and performed strange penances.　The rich people grew profuse and penitent, and poverty, always honourable among Jews, came in those strange days to be fashionable.

And now, so heralded, and in truth so advertised, for what a bill-posting agency would do for similar worthies in this generation a certain Nathan Benjamin of Jerusalem seems to have done in clumsier fashion for Sabbathai, their hero was among them.　Nathan, it is to be feared, was less of a convert than a colleague of our prophet, but to tear-dimmed eyes which saw visions, to starved hearts which by reason of sorrow judged in hunger and in weakness, prophet and partner both loomed heroic.　It is curious, when one thinks of it, that the same race which had been critical over a Moses should have been credulous over a Sabbathai Zevi.　Is it a possible explanation that the art of making bricks without straw, however difficult of acquirement, being at any rate of the nature of healthy, outdoor employment, was less depressing in its results on character than the cumulative effect of centuries of Ghetto-bounded toil?　Something, too, may be allowed for the fact that the Promised Land lay then in prospect and now in retrospect.　Altogether, perhaps, it may be urged in this instance that the idol does not quite give an accurate measure of the worshipper. A Deliverer was at their doors, a Deliverer from worse than Egyptian bondage; that was all that this poor deluded people could stop to think, and out they rushed in ludicrous, reverent welcome of a light that was not dawn. With a fine appreciation of effect, Sabbathai gently put aside the rich embroidered cloths that were spread beneath his feet; and this subtle indication of humility, and of a desire to tread the dusty paths with his brethren, gained him many a wavering adherent. For there were waverers. Even amidst all the enthusiasm, there was now and then an awkward question asked, for these shabby traders of Smyrna were all of them more or less learned in the Law and the Prophets, and though their tired hearts could accept this blustering, unideal presentment of the Prince of Peace, yet their minds and memories made occasional protest concerning dates and circumstances. And presently one Samuel Pennia, a man of some local reputation, took heart of grace, and preached and proclaimed with a hundred most obvious arguments that Sabbathai had no smallest claim to the titles he was arrogantly assuming. Law and logic too were on Pennia's side; and yet, strange and incomprehensible as it seems to sober retro-

spect, he failed to convince even himself.
After discussions innumerable and of the
stormiest sort, Pennia began to doubt and to
hesitate, and finally he and all his family
became strenuous and, there is no reason to
doubt, honest supporters of Sabbathai. Still
the tumults which had been provoked, though
they could not rouse the multitude to a doubt
of their Deliverer, did awake in them a desire
that he should deign to demonstrate his power
to unbelievers, and a cry, comic or pathetic as
we take it, broke forth for a miracle—a simultaneous prayer for something, anything, super-
natural. It was embarrassing; and Sabbathai,
one old chronicler gravely remarks, was
'horribly puzzled for a miracle.' But in a
moment the cynical humour of the man came
to his help, and where the true prophet, in
honest humility, might have hesitated, with
' Lord, I cannot speak; I am a child,' on his
lips, our charlatan was ready and self-possessed
and equal to the occasion. With solemn gait
and rapt gaze, which, as a contemporary record
expresses it, he had ' starcht on,' Sabbathai
stood for some seconds silent; then, suddenly
throwing up his hands to heaven, ' Behold!'
he exclaimed in thrilling accents, 'see you
not yon pillar of fire?' And the expectant
crowd turned, and in their eager, almost
hysterical, excitement many believed they

saw, and many, who did not see, doubted their sight and not the vision. Those who looked and looked in vain were silent, hardly daring to own that to their unworthy eyes the blessed assurance had been denied. So Sabbathai returned to his home in triumph. No further miracles were asked or needed, and doubters in his Messiahship were henceforth accounted by the synagogue as heretics and infidels and fit subjects for excommunication. In his character of prophet no religious ceremonial was henceforth considered complete without the presence of Sabbathai, and in his character of prince and leader unlimited wealth was at his command. Here, however, came in the one redeeming point. Sabbathai's ambition had no taint of avarice about it. He took of no man's gold and of no woman's jewels, though both were laid unstintingly at his feet. And then, suddenly, at this period of his greatest success, subtly appreciating, it may be, the wisdom of taking fortune at the flood, Sabbathai announced his intention of leaving Smyrna, and the month of January, 1667, saw him embark in a small coasting-vessel bound for Constantinople. Here a reception altogether unexpected and unprophesied was awaiting him. There had been great weeping and lamentation among the disciples he left, and there was proportionately great rejoicing

among the larger community his presence was
to favour, for, by virtue of the curious system
of intercommunication which has always prevailed among the dispersed race, the news of
Sabbathai's movements and intentions spread
quickly and in ever-widening circles. It reached
at length some ears which had not been
reckoned upon, and penetrated to a brain
which had preserved its balance. The
Sultan of Turkey, Mahomet IV., heard of
this expected visitor to his capital, and
when, after nine-and-thirty days of stormy
passage, the sea-sick prophet was entering
the port, the first thing he saw was two
State barges, fully manned, putting out to
meet him. It may be hoped that he was too
sea-sick to indulge in any audible predictions,
or to put in sonorous words any bright dream
born of that brief glimpse of a brother poten-
tate hastening to greet his spiritual sovereign.
For any such prophecy would have been all
too rudely and too quickly falsified. It was
as prisoner, not as prophet, that Sabbathai
was to enter Constantinople, and a dungeon,
not a palace, was his destination. The Sultan
had indeed heard of the worse than mid-
summer madness that had seized on his
Jewish subjects throughout the Turkish
Empire, and he proceeded to stay the
plague with a prompt high-handedness which

a Grand Vizier out of *The Arabian Nights* could hardly have excelled. For two long months Sabbathai was kept a close prisoner in uncomfortable quarters in Constantinople, and was from thence transferred to a cell in the Castle of Abydos. Of the effects of this imperial reception on the prophet himself we shall judge in the sequel, but its effects on his followers were, strange to say, not at all depressing. To these faithful deluded folks their hero behind prison bars gained only a halo of martyrdom. Was it not fitting that the Servant of Israel should be 'acquainted with grief'? The dangerous sentiment of pity added itself to the passion of love and faith, and pilgrims from all parts—Poland, Venice, Amsterdam—hurried to the city as if it were a shrine. Sabbathai took up the *rôle*, and by gentle proclamation bestowed the blessings and the promises which had been hitherto showered down in set speeches. And so the madness grew, till a sordid element crept into it, and at first, curiously enough, this also increased it. In the crowd, thus attracted to the neighbourhood, the Turks saw an opportunity for making money. The price of lodging and provision for the pilgrims was constantly raised, and by degrees a sight of Sabbathai or a word from him came to be quite a source of income to his guards. The necessary element of secrecy about such transactions acted, both directly and indirectly, as fuel to the flames. The Jews in the spread of the faith and in their immunity from persecution saw Divine interposition, while the Turks naturally favoured Sabbathai's pretensions, and continued to raise their prices to each new batch of believers. But complaints were bound in time to reach headquarters. The overcrowding and excitement was a danger to the Turkish inhabitants of Constantinople, and among the Jews themselves Sabbathai's success begat at length a more disturbing element than doubt. A rival Messiah came forward in a certain Nehemiah Cohen, a learned rabbi from Poland. A sort of twin Messiahship seems first to have suggested itself to these worthies. Nehemiah, under the title of Ben Ephraim, was to fulfil the probationary part of the prophecies on the subject, and Sabbathai, as Ben David, to take the triumphant close and climax. So much was agreed upon, when Sabbathai, who was still a prisoner, became a little apprehensive of a possible change of parts by Nehemiah, who was at large. Disputes ensued, and ended in an appeal by Sabbathai to the community. A renewed vote of confidence in their native hero was recorded, and Nehemiah's claims to a partnership were altogether and summarily rejected. His own pretensions thus disallowed, Nehemiah at once turned round and hastened to denounce the insincerity of the whole affair to such of the Turkish officials as would listen to him. He was backed up by a very few of the wise men of his own community who had managed to keep their honest doubts in spite of the general madness; and presently by much effort a messenger was despatched to Adrianople, where Mahomet IV. was holding his Court, with full particulars of Sabbathai's latest doings. The Sultan listened to the story, and was literally and ludicrously true to the strictest traditional ideal of what one may call the sack and bowstring system, and there is no doubt that, in this instance, substantial justice was secured by it.

Without excuse or ceremonial of any sort, without farewell from the friends he left or greetings from the curious throng which awaited him, Sabbathai was hurried into Adrianople, and within an hour of his arrival, deposited, limp and apprehensive, in the presence-chamber. The giant's robe seemed to be slipping visibly from his shaking shoulders as, sternly desired to give an account of himself, he, the glib cosmopolitan prophet, begged for an interpreter. Without comment on this sudden and surprising failure in the gift of tongues the request was granted; and patiently, silently, Court and Sultan stroked their beards and listened to the marvellous tale which was unfolded. Were they doubtful, or convinced? Was he after all to triumph? It almost seemed so as the story ended, and the expectant hush was broken by the Sultan quietly requesting a miracle. Wild thoughts of a lucky stroke of legerdemain, which should recover all, must have instantly occurred to this other-world adventurer. But no audaciously summoned pillar of fire would here have served his turn; the astute Sultan meant to choose his own miracle.

'Thou shalt not be afraid . . . of the arrow that flieth by day. A thousand shall fall at thy side and ten thousand at thy right hand, but it shall not come nigh unto thee.' In the most literal and most liberal meaning the pseudo-prophet was requested to interpret these words of his national poet. He was to strip, said the Sultan, and to let the archers shoot at him, and thus make manifest in his own flesh his confidence in his own assumptions.

Not for one moment did Sabbathai hesitate. A man's behaviour at a supreme crisis in his life is not determined by the sudden need. It is not to a single, sudden trumpet-

call that character responds, but to the tone
set by daily uncounted matin and evensong.
Sabbathai was as incapable of the heroic
death as of the heroic life. It had been all
a game to him; the people's passionate enthusiasm, that pitiful power of theirs for
seeing visions, were just points in the game—
points in his favour. And now the game was
lost; he was cool enough to realise this at a
glance, and to seize upon the one move which
he might yet make to his own advantage.
With a startling burst of calculated candour
he owned to it all, that he was no prophet,
no Saviour, no willing 'witness' even; only
a historical Jew, and very much at the Sultan's
service.

Mahomet smiled. The tragedy of the situation was for the Jews; the comedy, and it
must have been irresistible, was his. Then
after due pause he gravely proceeded, that
insomuch as Sabbathai's pretensions to Palestine were an infringement on Turkish vested
rights in that province, the repentant prophet
must give an earnest of his recovered loyalty
as a Turkish subject by turning Turk and
abjuring Judaism altogether. And cheer-
fully enough Sabbathai assented, audaciously
adding that such a change had been long desired by him, and that he eagerly and respect-
fully welcomed this opportunity of making

his first profession of faith as a Mahometan in the presence of Mahomet's namesake and temporal representative.

And thus the scene, at which one knows not whether to laugh or cry, was over; and when the curtain rises again it is on the merest and most exasperating commonplace— on Sabbathai, fat and turbaned, living and dying as a respectable Turk. For the actors behind the scenes, there was never any call, neither to hail a Saviour nor to mourn a martyr. For them, this puzzling bit of passion-play was just a mirage in the wilderness of their lives; and for many and many a weary year foolish and faithful folk debated whether it was mirage or reality. For his dupes survived him, this sorry impostor of the seventeenth century; and their illusion, hoping all things, believing all things, withered into delusion and died hard. Such faculty perhaps, for all its drawbacks, gives staying-power to man or nation. It is where there is no vision that the people perish.

NOW AND THEN

A COMPOSITE SKETCH

'THE old order changeth, giving place to new,' and many and bewildering have been such changes since the daughters of Zelophehad trooped down before the elders of Israel to plead for women's rights. The claim of those five fatherless, husbandless sisters to ' have a possession among the brethren of our father' has been brought, and has been answered since in a thousand different ways, but the chivalrous spirit in which it was met then seems, in a subtle sort of way, to symbolise the attitude of Israel to unprotected woman-hood, and to suggest the type of character which ensured such ready and respectful consideration. It is curious and interesting in these modern days to take up what Heine called the 'family chronicle of the Jews,' and to find, as in a long gallery of family portraits, the type repeating itself through every variety of 'treatment' and costume. Clear and distinct they stand out, the long line of our

M

Jewish maids and matrons, not 'faultily fault-
less' by any means, yet presenting in their
vigorous lovableness a delightful continuity
of wholesome womanhood, an unbroken line
of fit claimants for fitting woman's rights.

Foremost among all heroines of all love
tales comes, of course, she whose long wooing
seemed 'but as a few days' to her young
lover, so strong and so steadfast was the
worship she won.   To the young, that maiden
'by the well's mouth' will stand always for
favourite text and familiar illustration, but to
older folks the sad-eyed *mater dolorosa* of the
Old Testament is to the full as interesting
and as suggestive an ideal.   One pictures her
with sackcloth for sole couch and covering
spread upon the bare rocks, selfless and tire-
less, through the heat of early harvest days
till chill autumn rains 'dropped upon them,'
scaring 'the birds of the air and the beasts
of the field' from her unburied dead.   And
then, as corrective to the pathos of Rizpah
and the romance of Rachel, the sweet, homely
figure of Ruth is at hand to suggest a whole
volume of virtues of the comfortable, everyday
sort; the one character, perhaps, in all story
who ever addressed an impassioned outburst of
affection to her mother-in-law, and then lived
up to it.   But the solitariness of the circumstance notwithstanding, and for all the fact

that she was a Moabitess born, Ruth, in the
practical nature of her good qualities, is a
typical Jewish heroine.   For what strikes one
most in the record of these long ago dead
women is that there is so much sense in their
sentiment, so much backbone to their gentle-
ness and simple-mindedness.   They do little
things in a great way instead of attacking
great things feebly.   Their womanhood in
its entire naturalness belongs to no especial
school, fits in to no especial groove of thought.
The same peg serves for a Solomon or a
Wordsworth, for an aphorism or a sonnet.
The woman whose 'price was above rubies,'
and she who was

> 'Not too great or good
> For human nature's daily food,'

might either have stood for the other's likeness; and if the test of poetry be, as Goethe
says, the substance which remains when the
poetry is reduced to prose, the test of an ideal
woman may be perhaps how she would translate into reality.   The 'family chronicle' stands
the test, and a dozen instances of it at once
occur to memory.   Michal, with her husband
in danger, does not wait to weep nor to
exclaim, but, strong of heart as of hand, helps
him to escape, and, ready of resource, by her
quick, deft arrangement of the bedchamber,

gains time to baffle his pursuers. Hannah, for all her holy enthusiasm, is mindful of the bodily needs of her embryo prophet, and as she comes with her husband to offer the 'yearly sacrifice' at Shiloh, brings with her the 'little coat' which she has made for the boy, and which, we may be quite sure, she has remembered to make a little bigger each time. Nor less, in her far-sighted scheming for her favourite son, is Rebekah heedless of 'human nature's daily food.' For all her concentration of thought on great issues she remembers to make ready 'the savoury meat such as his father loved' before she sends Jacob to the critical interview. It is altogether with something of a shock that we ponder on that curious development. The scheming, unscrupulous wife seems quite other than the simple country maiden with her quick assent to the grave young husband whom she was able to 'comfort after his mother's death.' Was that pretty, frank 'I will go' of hers only unconventional, one wonders, or perhaps just a trifle unfeeling, foreshadowing in the young girl, so ready to leave her home, a rather rootless state of affections, an Undine-like indifference to old ties? That touch of the carefully prepared dinner at any rate makes us smile as we sigh, putting us *fin de siècle* folks, as it does, in touch with tent life, and

keeping the traditions of home influence un-
altered through the ages.

In Lord Burleigh's *Precepts to his Son for
the Well-Ordering of a Man's Life*, occurs the
direction, 'Thou wilt find to thy great grief
there is nothing more fulsome than a she-
fool.' It is an axiom almost as pregnant of
meaning as its author's famous nod, and seems
to suggest as possible that the proverbial
harmony of the Jewish domestic circle may be
in a measure due to its comparative immunity
from she-fools. The women of Israel, *pur
sang*, it is certain, are rarely noisy or assertive,
and have at all times been more ready to
realise their responsibilities than their 'rights.'
In their woman's kingdom, comprehending its
limits and not wasting its opportunities, they
have been content to reign and not to govern,
and neither exceptional power nor exceptional
intellect have affected this position. The
pretty young Queen of Persia, we read, for all
her new dignities, 'did the commandment of
Mordecai as when she was brought up with
him,' and Miriam with her timbrel and
Deborah under her palm - tree might have
been unconscious illustrative anachronisms of
a very profound saying, so well content were
they to 'make their country's songs' and to
leave it to Moses to 'make the laws.' The
one-man rule has been always fully and freely

acknowledged in Israel, and in the ideal sketch as in the real portraits of its woman-kind, her 'husband,' her 'children,' her 'clothing,' and the 'ways of her household' are supreme features. 'To do a man,' one man, 'good and not evil all the days of his life,' may seem to modern maidens a some-what limited ambition, but it is just to remember that to this typical woman comes full permission to indulge in her 'own works' and encouragement 'to speak with merchants from afar,' a habit this, one ventures to think, which would open up even to Girton and Newnham graduates extended powers of conversation and correspondence in their own and foreign languages. And, withal, that pretty saying of an elderly and prosaic Rabbi, 'I do not call my wife, wife, but home,' has poetry and practicality too, to recommend it. For in so far as there is truth in the dictum, that 'men will be always what women please, that if we want men to be great and good, we must teach women what greatness and goodness are,' there really seems a good deal to be said for the old-fashioned type we have been considering, and certainly some comfort to be found in the fact that against the *ewig weibliche* time itself is powerless. Realities may shift and vary, but ideals for the most part stand fast, and thus, despite all superficial differences, in essentials the situation is unchanged between those daughters of the desert and our daughters of to-day.   Now, as then, the claim is allowed to a rightful 'possession among their brethren.'

Printed by T. and A. CONSTABLE, Printers to Her Majesty
at the Edinburgh University Press

www.ingramcontent.com/pod-product-compliance
Lightning Source LLC
Chambersburg PA
CBHW030843270326
41928CB00007B/1193